Analytic Philosophy: A Very Short Introduction

Very Short Introductions available now:

ACCOUNTING Christopher Nobes
ADOLESCENCE Peter K. Smith
ADVERTISING Winston Fletcher
AFRICAN AMERICAN RELIGION
    Eddie S. Glaude Jr
AFRICAN HISTORY John Parker and
    Richard Rathbone
AFRICAN RELIGIONS Jacob K. Olupona
AGEING Nancy A. Pachana
AGNOSTICISM Robin Le Poidevin
AGRICULTURE Paul Brassley and
    Richard Soffe
ALEXANDER THE GREAT
    Hugh Bowden
ALGEBRA Peter M. Higgins
AMERICAN HISTORY Paul S. Boyer
AMERICAN IMMIGRATION
    David A. Gerber
AMERICAN LEGAL HISTORY
    G. Edward White
AMERICAN POLITICAL HISTORY
    Donald Critchlow
AMERICAN POLITICAL PARTIES
    AND ELECTIONS L. Sandy Maisel
AMERICAN POLITICS
    Richard M. Valelly
THE AMERICAN PRESIDENCY
    Charles O. Jones
THE AMERICAN REVOLUTION
    Robert J. Allison
AMERICAN SLAVERY
    Heather Andrea Williams
THE AMERICAN WEST Stephen Aron
AMERICAN WOMEN'S HISTORY
    Susan Ware

ANAESTHESIA Aidan O'Donnell
ANALYTIC PHILOSOPHY
    Michael Beaney
ANARCHISM Colin Ward
ANCIENT ASSYRIA Karen Radner
ANCIENT EGYPT Ian Shaw
ANCIENT EGYPTIAN ART AND
    ARCHITECTURE Christina Riggs
ANCIENT GREECE Paul Cartledge
THE ANCIENT NEAR EAST
    Amanda H. Podany
ANCIENT PHILOSOPHY Julia Annas
ANCIENT WARFARE
    Harry Sidebottom
ANGELS David Albert Jones
ANGLICANISM Mark Chapman
THE ANGLO-SAXON AGE
    John Blair
ANIMAL BEHAVIOUR
    Tristram D. Wyatt
THE ANIMAL KINGDOM
    Peter Holland
ANIMAL RIGHTS David DeGrazia
THE ANTARCTIC Klaus Dodds
ANTISEMITISM Steven Beller
ANXIETY Daniel Freeman and
    Jason Freeman
THE APOCRYPHAL GOSPELS
    Paul Foster
ARCHAEOLOGY Paul Bahn
ARCHITECTURE Andrew Ballantyne
ARISTOCRACY William Doyle
ARISTOTLE Jonathan Barnes
ART HISTORY Dana Arnold
ART THEORY Cynthia Freeland

Available soon:

For more information visit our website

www.oup.com/vsi/

Michael Beaney

ANALYTIC
PHILOSOPHY

A Very Short Introduction

OXFORD

UNIVERSITY PRESS

Great Clarendon Street, Oxford, OX2 6DP,
United Kingdom

Oxford University Press is a department of the University of Oxford.
It furthers the University's objective of excellence in research, scholarship,
and education by publishing worldwide. Oxford is a registered trade mark of
Oxford University Press in the UK and in certain other countries

© Michael Beaney 2017

The moral rights of the author have been asserted

First edition published in 2017

Published in the United States of America by Oxford University Press
198 Madison Avenue, New York, NY 10016, United States of America

British Library Cataloguing in Publication Data
Data available

Library of Congress Control Number: 2017945749

ISBN 978-0-19-877802-8

Printed and bound by CPI Group (UK) Ltd, Croydon, CR0 4YY

Contents

Preface and acknowledgements

This is a book that I have wanted to write for quite a while—a book that seeks to introduce analytic philosophy to those beginning their study of philosophy, and to anyone interested in knowing what has been going on in philosophy over the last century or so and what 'analytic philosophy', in particular, means. But it was only once I had finished editing *The Oxford Handbook of the History of Analytic Philosophy*, which was published in 2013, that I felt ready to do so. The *Handbook* contains thirty-nine chapters, covering the whole history of analytic philosophy from its origins in the 19th century to the most recent work, across as many fields as it was possible to include in a single volume. In email correspondence with the contributors in planning the volume and in reading their chapters, I gained a stronger sense of what analytic philosophy involves, and of both its strengths and weaknesses. Some, perhaps all, may disagree with one or more features of the account that I offer here; but I would like to thank them all—as well as the many others with whom I have discussed analytic philosophy over the years—for helping to shape my views. Naming them all here would conflict with the very shortness of this introduction, but I did so in my preface to the *Handbook*.

I lectured on early analytic philosophy in Peking University in the winter semester of 2011, and have taught further courses and given talks on analytic philosophy at various other universities in

China since then. I was struck by the keen interest in analytic philosophy that has been growing rapidly in China in recent years, and I learnt a lot, not just about what needs explaining by the challenging questions I was asked, but also about Chinese ways of thinking. I have partly written this book with a Chinese audience in mind, in the hope that it will contribute to deepening the dialogue with Chinese ideas and philosophers—and non-Western thinking, generally—that is very much needed today.

As I was preparing the final version of this book, I was giving an introductory lecture course on analytic philosophy at the Humboldt University of Berlin, open to all students of the university and the wider public, and drawing on ideas in this book. Teaching and working in a bilingual context has also helped me appreciate what aspects of analytic philosophy need explaining, defending, and criticizing. I would like to thank all my students—both in Berlin and in all the other places I have taught, mainly in England, over the last thirty years—for providing the stimulus to my teaching and writing about analytic philosophy. In my introductory chapter to the *Handbook*, I offered a gloss on the lines from Alexander Pope that I also quote in Chapter 3 of the present book: if an idea is worth thinking, then it is worth saying clearly; and if it is said clearly, then it will crystallize thinking in others. The sentiment expressed here has always informed my teaching and writing, and I have sought to realize it here.

I have had excellent support and encouragement from the staff at OUP. Andrea Keegan read two early drafts of the first chapters and the original proposal, and was extremely helpful in suggesting how it could be improved. Jenny Nugee steered it through the final stages, Erica Martin organized the illustrations, and Klara Smith drew the pictures that I am delighted to have in the book. Two anonymous external readers read the Introduction and first two chapters at proposal stage, and one of them also read the whole version at the penultimate stage, as did a further reader from OUP. Joy Mellor did a very efficient job as copy-editor, as did

Dorothy McCarthy in proof-reading and Saraswathi Ethiraju in overseeing the production of the book. I would like to thank all of them for their contribution to its final form.

Various family members and friends have also read drafts of chapters of this book at different stages. I am especially grateful to Sharon Macdonald, our three children Harriet, Thomas, and Tara, Bob Clark, and Anna Bellomo for comments. I also thank Sharon for taking the photo that appears in Chapter 6 and Cate Kay for allowing the use of her car. I dedicate this book to my present and future grandchildren—to Iris, to the new one on the way as I write, and to those that may come along later (who knows?). It distils a lot of what I have thought about over the last forty years, and, indeed, of me—and I hope that this book, at least, will be short enough for them to read it when their intellectual curiosity is aroused.

List of illustrations

Introduction

Many professional philosophers working today would describe themselves as 'analytic philosophers'. Certainly, this is true of many philosophers teaching in colleges and universities in the English-speaking world. But analytic philosophy has been growing rapidly elsewhere: one sign of this is the establishment over the last twenty years or so of societies for analytic philosophy right across the world, from East Asia to Latin America. This is not to say that there is agreement on what 'analytic philosophy' means or what its main concerns, methods, and successes are. But I hope that this book will give you some idea of what it involves and of its achievements and strengths, as well as of its limitations and weaknesses.

One claim that is often made about analytic philosophy is that it places great emphasis on clarity, precision, and rigour: clarity of thinking, precision of expression, and rigour of argumentation. Analytic philosophers try to get as clear as they can about the philosophical issues that they address, to express their ideas as precisely as possible (using both ordinary language and technical vocabulary, as appropriate), and to present their arguments with the maximum degree of rigour (often using formal logic). I think that clarity, precision, and rigour are indeed cardinal intellectual virtues, and I have attempted to embody them in this book (though I have minimized the use of formal logic). How successful

I have been will be for you to judge. But even if I have not been as successful as I would have liked, I hope that you will at least see why these virtues are prized.

Clarity, precision, and rigour are not the only intellectual virtues, however. Creativity, fruitfulness, and systematicity are just three others that might be mentioned. I think the best analytic philosophy also exhibits these virtues, although this might be better appreciated. All good philosophy, in my view, is *conceptually creative*: it gives us new conceptual resources to think more carefully and deeply about things, which can in turn lead to fruitful applications and the development of more systematic theories. Analytic philosophy has not been known for its system-building in the grand style of some of the philosophers of the past. On the contrary, it has often been associated with a piecemeal approach: small problems are broken off to be chewed away at one by one. The danger here is that it is then easy to lose sight of the wood for the trees, a criticism that might indeed be made of some analytic philosophy today. Yet the systematic nature of analytic philosophy and of its underlying motivations, in particular, also deserves greater recognition. So a further aim of the present book is to give some sense both of the conceptual creativity of analytic philosophy and of the bigger picture in which its fruitfulness and systematic ambitions can be appreciated.

Philosophical questions

One way to introduce analytic philosophy is to take the question that we will explore in detail in Chapter 1: how many things are there in the world? The question is easy to ask. As soon as a child has learnt to count and to use the words 'thing' and 'world', they might come up with it (most likely when they are being put to bed). But could such a question have an answer? Does it even make sense? The question is not an isolated example. There are many others. Where was I before I was conceived? How long did it take to create the world? Do numbers exist? Is '2 + 2 = 4' true everywhere? Is 'This sentence is false' true or false? Do I have free will? All these questions are easy to ask, and it is natural to think that they must have answers, just because they are similar to questions that do have answers—'Where was I before I moved to Berlin?', 'How long did it take to write this book?', 'Do pandas exist?', and so on. But it is by no means obvious what the answers are, if indeed they do have answers.

If such questions do not have answers, then are they meaningless? They do not seem meaningless, since we understand the words used in asking them and the questions are grammatically well formed. And even if we described them as meaningless, this would only be the start of explaining why they are different from the similar questions that have straightforward answers. Why are they meaningless? What distinguishes them from the similar ones that do have meaning? What do we mean by 'meaning'? What is the connection between having an answer and having a meaning?

Questions that do not admit of straightforward answers, and yet seem as if they should, are characteristic of philosophy. Some of them might indeed turn out to have answers, as science progresses to provide the conceptual resources and empirical data to do so. But others remain intractable and continue to give rise to philosophical puzzlement. Inventive 'answers' can always be offered. Where was I before I was conceived? A twinkle in my parents' eyes? This is only a metaphor. In God's mind? Here we would need some heavy-duty theology to fill this out, if it can be done at all. In the body of some other human or non-human animal who died before I was born? Here we would have to appeal to some doctrine of reincarnation.

Such inventive answers only highlight the oddity or intractability of the questions. Such questions have been asked throughout the history of human thought—indeed, as just suggested, many of them seem to arise naturally as soon as language has the relevant words and grammatical structure. Answers have also been given

3

throughout the history of human thought, not least by philosophers, but it is only relatively recently—in the 20th century—that philosophers have approached these questions with attention to the workings of language and awareness of the multifarious ways in which language can mislead us. It is this approach that is characteristic of what has come to be called 'analytic philosophy', especially as it developed in the first half of the 20th century. We will address the question of how and why analytic philosophy acquired its name in the final chapter of this book, after we have seen some examples of what is involved. The obvious thing to say, though, is that analytic philosophy is called 'analytic' because of the emphasis placed on analysis. But this just raises the question of what is meant by 'analysis', and what forms of analysis are employed in analytic philosophy. This, too, is only best explained by examples, and we will consider a range of different examples in what follows.

Thought-thinking

In considering these examples, what I want to do, above all, is engage you in the *activity* of analytic philosophizing. Analytic philosophy has its fair share of intellectual landmarks. But my aim is not to be your guide on a sight-seeing tour but your minder (as it might best be called here!) on a thought-thinking trip. In seeking to engage you in actual philosophizing, I shall introduce you on the way to some of the key ideas of five of the founders of the analytic tradition: Gottlob Frege (1848–1925), Bertrand Russell (1872–1970), G. E. Moore (1873–1958), Ludwig Wittgenstein (1889–1951), and Susan Stebbing (1885–1943). Each of the main themes of the five chapters that follow has been chosen to do just this. But we will only explore those ideas that are relevant to the theme. The chapters should not be seen as giving a rounded account of their respective philosophies. We will encounter ideas of other philosophers, too, but in a book of this kind, it would be impossible to do justice to these as well. There are plenty of accounts of their ideas available, from summaries in encyclopedias to scholarly monographs. We will indulge in a little sight-seeing in the final chapter, though, and some suggestions for further reading are made at the end of this book.

Before we begin our trip, however, let me issue one piece of travel advice. If you are new to analytic philosophy, then you will not understand what we are doing without acquiring certain concepts. Without the relevant concepts, we cannot even think certain thoughts, so if the aim is to give you these thoughts, then the concepts must be grasped. Some of these concepts, such as the concept of an object's falling under a concept or the concept of being self-identical, may seem strange when first encountered, but they are relatively straightforward once explained. Others, such as the concept of a concept itself or the concept of meaning, may seem familiar, but they will need to be understood in more precise or technical ways. Other concepts may be entirely new, such as the concept of a transfinite number. So if, as you are reading this book, you do not initially grasp a concept, then be patient. Sometimes you may need to re-read a paragraph. Reading philosophy is not like reading a novel. You will have to slow down, re-read, and even stop at times to reflect before going on. Sometimes you will need to see what work the concept does before starting to grasp it, and then you can go back to the initial explanation to consolidate your understanding. As I said at the beginning, analytic philosophy—like all good philosophy—is conceptually creative, and like all good creative activities, its originality and value may not be immediately recognized. But if you persevere, then the richer conceptual resources and refined reasoning skills you will acquire will open up a whole new realm of intellectual thought.

Chapter 1

How many things are there?

How many things are there in the world? If you ask me how many children I have, I can immediately answer you: three. If you ask me how many books there are in my office, I could tell you, though I would have to count them. If you ask me how old I am in minutes, I could work it out, though I would have to check with my mother what precise time I was born. If you ask me how many cells I have in my body, I would have to consult a biologist and could only give an approximate answer, taking into account such factors as my weight. But can we answer the question 'How many things are there *altogether* in the world?' Could we count them all, at least in principle, or work it out? And if we couldn't give the exact number, could we at least give an approximate answer?

Things and kinds of things

If we find the question 'How many things are there in the world?' intractable or perplexing or meaningless or plain silly, is it because the world is just too large to give any sensible answer? If so, then let us take a simpler question: How many things are there in my study? We might think that all I need to do here is look around and count them. I might start by counting my books. But if I now take one of these books, should I count each page separately? Should I also count the words on each page? Is my armchair one thing or two things—e.g., the wooden frame and the cushion—or many things? Is my desk one thing or five things (the top and the four legs into which it can be dismantled)? The question cannot be answered until we specify what *kinds of things* we have in mind. If *books* or *chairs* or *desks*—or indeed *books or chairs or desks* (taking them together)—are meant, then I can give you the answer, at least in principle, or approximately. But to ask how many things there are altogether, without such specification, seems to lack an answer.

But is the question therefore meaningless? In particular contexts, it may indeed have meaning. Imagine that I am moving house, and I phone up a removals company to request a quotation. As we go through the rooms one by one, I am asked how many things I have in my study. Here I might reply: 'Well, I have about 1,000 books, one desk, three chairs, a sofa, an armchair, two filing cabinets, a coffee table, and five potted plants.' It would be misleading to summarize this by saying that I have 1,014 things (adding them all up), but it is an appropriate reply. This only reinforces the point, though, that we need to specify the *kinds of things* that are meant in giving an answer to such a question. What the removals person meant by 'things' are all those physical objects that would need to be carried away, whether singly or packed up in boxes. In answering the question, I would have to specify the kinds of things relevant for providing a quotation—for example, to work out how many boxes would be needed for my books.

The context, then, can often make clear what kinds of things are meant in asking 'How many things are there?'. If not, then all one can say is 'It depends on what you mean by "thing"'. That would place the onus on the questioner to specify what they meant. Returning now to the more general question 'How many things are there in the world?', it is hard to see what context might give such a question a clear enough sense to have an answer. But if it were indeed to have a sense, then it would have to be specified what kinds of things were meant (atoms? molecules? chemical elements?); and this is the crucial point.

This already illustrates one form that 'analysis' takes in philosophy. If it is not immediately obvious how to answer a given question, then we need to identify its possible meanings. Perhaps we will find the intended or relevant meaning by understanding the context; but if we don't, and we want to explain how the question might therefore only *seem* meaningful, then we may need to *imagine* possible contexts in which the question has an answer. Only when we have established that none of these possible contexts is the actual context are we entitled to conclude that, on this occasion, the question is meaningless and hence unanswerable. Understood as just a form of words, any question may have multiple possible meanings, and analysis is required to distinguish the relevant ones. This is 'analysis' not in the crude sense of simply 'decomposing' something already given, but in the sense of identifying all the relevant possibilities—a process that requires imagination. Analysis is far more creative than is often thought.

Introducing Gottlob Frege

Gottlob Frege (1848–1925) is now widely acknowledged as one of the main founders of analytic philosophy. He was born in Wismar, on the Mecklenburg coast in north-east Germany, studied at the Universities of Jena and Göttingen, and spent his entire academic career back at the University of Jena teaching mathematics. His central concern was with the nature of mathematics and, in particular, of arithmetic. What are numbers, and how do we gain knowledge of arithmetic? Attempting to answer these questions made Frege as much a philosopher as a mathematician. His answer is easy to state, though much more difficult to justify (as Frege was to find to his cost), and only a little less difficult to explain—though I will do my best in this chapter. Arithmetic, according to Frege, is essentially a form of logic—a view that has come to be called 'logicism'—and numbers are a kind of logical object. To show this, Frege had to develop logical theory, and this made him a logician as well as a mathematician and philosopher.

Indeed, the basis of his status as one of the founders of analytic philosophy is as the creator of modern logic—of what we now know as *quantificational logic*. He called his logical system 'Begriffsschrift' (literally, 'concept-script'), which he first presented in a short book published under that name in 1879.

Frege's most accessible book, now generally regarded as a philosophical masterpiece, is *The Foundations of Arithmetic*, published in 1884. Central to his account is his claim that number statements are assertions about concepts. We are already in a position to understand this claim. Take our earlier example of a book—let us say, the book you are now reading. How many things do we have here? One book or 150 pages or 38,000 words (approximately)? Clearly the answer depends on the kind of thing we have in mind or, as we might now put it, the *concept* by means of which we are thinking of it. If we are conceiving of it as a book, then the answer is one; if as a set of pages, then the answer is 150; and if as a collection of words, then the answer is 38,000.

Consider a number statement—for example, that this book has 150 pages. According to Frege, we are attributing the number 150 not to the object itself (this book) but to the concept "page of this book". (In what follows, concepts will be referred to by using double inverted commas.) This concept has 150 instances. The statement, in other words, is not about the object that it appears to be about (reflected in the fact that 'this book' is the grammatical subject of the sentence we use to make the statement), but about the concept that we have to grasp in order to do the relevant counting. On Frege's view, what 'The book has 150 pages' really means is 'The concept "page of this book" has 150 instances'. We will return to the idea of what a sentence 'really means' in Chapter 3. The key point here is the illustration of Frege's central claim that number statements are assertions about concepts.

If Frege is right, then we have already made progress in answering one of the apparently simplest but actually trickiest questions in the history of philosophy. What are numbers? Let us restrict ourselves here to the numbers that we use for counting, the so-called natural numbers: 0, 1, 2, 3, and so on. We can only count something when we have a concept by means of which to think of it. Something can be one book, or 150 pages, or 38,000 words; it is only when we understand the relevant concept that we can determine the number. Once stated, this might seem obvious, but it is an important insight and suggests a conclusion that might be put as follows. It is not things in themselves to which numbers are assigned but the concepts by means of which we think of things. For present purposes, we can regard concepts as representing properties of things: something can be a book or a page or a word, for example. Numbers can then be regarded as properties of properties. (As we will see, this is only a first approximation to Frege's view, but it is on the right lines.) The property of being this book has itself the property of having one instance; the property of being a page of this book has itself the property of having 150 instances; and so on.

Why was this important for Frege? The short answer is that the property of having an instance is a logical property, in other words, can be defined purely logically. We will come back to this in Chapter 2; but if we accept it, then we have already taken a step towards showing that number statements can be defined in logical terms.

Objects and concepts

Let us return to our main theme. To answer the question 'How many things are there?', we need to know what kinds of things are meant. In Frege's terminology, we need to understand the relevant concept to determine what number is applicable. In talking of *kinds of things* we are already presupposing a distinction between things and kinds of things. In Frege's terminology, this is the distinction between *objects* and *concepts*. Just as things can be classified into different kinds of things, and one thing can be classified in more than one way (something can be a horse as well as an animal), so too objects can be conceived by means of different concepts, and one and the same object can fall under different concepts.

The relation of an object's falling under a concept is regarded by Frege as the most fundamental logical relation of all. It forms the core of the simplest kind of thought we can have. Consider, for example, the thought that Gottlob is human. This involves thinking of something, namely Gottlob, as having a certain property, namely, the property of being human. Frege characterizes this as thinking that a particular object (Gottlob) falls under a particular concept (the concept "human"). For Frege, this relation cannot be analysed further and is the basis for more complex thoughts, such as the thought that all humans are mortal, which he characterizes as the thought that whatever object falls under the concept "human" also falls under the concept "mortal".

We can also have thoughts about concepts, such as the thought that the concept "page of this book" has 150 instances. Frege characterizes this as the thought that the concept "page of this book" falls within the concept "has 150 instances", where the concept "page of this book" is a *first-level concept* and the concept "has 150 instances" is a *second-level concept*. First-level concepts are concepts under which objects fall, and second-level concepts are concepts within which first-level concepts fall. (Frege distinguishes here between *falling under* and *falling within*, to bring out the difference of levels involved, but the two relations are analogous.) Number statements are thus to be analysed, on Frege's view, as stating of a first-level concept that it falls within a second-level concept, a second-level concept that ascribes a certain number of instances to the first-level concept. To say that this book has 150 pages is thus to say that the first-level concept "page of this book" falls within the second-level concept "has 150 instances".

We can also say things about second-level concepts, which requires third-level concepts, and so on. The concept "second-level concept" is an example of a third-level concept (since second-level concepts fall within it). On Frege's view, then, there is a hierarchy of concepts: first-level concepts, second-level concepts, third-level concepts, and so on. The question of how many things there are—even the most basic 'kinds of things'—is already beginning to look rather more complex than we might at first have assumed!

Extensions of concepts

The distinction between objects and concepts is the most fundamental distinction in Frege's philosophy (and similar distinctions have been drawn throughout the history of philosophy). But there is one more kind of thing that we need to introduce before we can return to the question of how many things there are. This is what Frege calls an 'extension of a concept', or, as it is also called, a 'class' or 'set'. Here the governing principle is that for every concept there is a class of things that fall under it. Take the concept "human", for example. Under this concept fall Gottlob Frege, Ludwig Wittgenstein, Susan Stebbing, and so on. These objects are members of the *class* of humans; in Frege's terminology, they belong to the extension of the concept "human". This class, according to Frege, is itself a kind of object, not a 'concrete' object but an 'abstract' object. 'Concrete' objects are the objects that exist in our empirical, spatio-temporal world; 'abstract' objects are the objects of our rational thought, whose 'existence' is another of those tricky questions that have plagued philosophers at least since Plato. More specifically, Frege regards classes as *logical* objects, since the idea of a class has traditionally been seen as logical, logic being understood as what governs our rational thought.

Let us go along with Frege for the time being and treat classes (extensions of concepts) as abstract, logical objects. (We will explore this idea further in Chapter 2.) Traditionally, numbers have also been seen as a type of abstract object. Frege certainly regarded them as objects rather than concepts. We talk of 'the number one', for example, indicating that it refers to an object, and when we say '2 is a square root of 4', this could be analysed as saying that the object 2 falls under the concept "square root of 4". So can numbers be regarded as *logical* objects? To answer 'yes', the obvious suggestion is to find appropriate classes with which to identify them, and this is what Frege did.

What are the natural numbers?

If we are going to define the natural numbers (0, 1, 2, 3, and so on) as classes, understood as logical objects, then we need to find appropriate logical concepts. Two of the most fundamental concepts of logic are the concepts of identity and of negation. Take the concept of identity, or more precisely, the concept of being identical with itself. Every object is identical with itself, in other words, every object falls under the concept "identical with itself". (It might be a strange thing to say, but seems to be trivially true.) So the corresponding class has as its members all objects. Now let us add the concept of negation to form the concept "not identical with itself". Nothing is not identical with itself. (If every object is identical with itself, then no object is not identical with itself. Again, this might be a strange thing to say, but seems to be trivially true.) So the corresponding class here has no members at all. This is what logicians call the 'null class' (or 'null set'), and in this case, it has been defined purely by means of logical concepts, as the class of things that are not self-identical.

The obvious suggestion is then to identify the first of the natural numbers, namely, the number 0, with the null class. This is what is done in modern set theory and is the simplest definition. Frege, in fact, offers a more complicated definition, identifying the number 0 not directly with the null class but with the class of classes that have the same number of members as the null class; but we can ignore this complication here. For present purposes, let us accept that this gives us our first natural number, the number 0, defined as the null class. We can then form the concept "is identical with 0" (i.e., the concept "is identical with the null class"). Here the corresponding class has just one member, namely, 0 (the null class itself), since only this object (i.e., 0) is identical with 0. This class (the class of things that are identical with 0) is distinct from its sole member (0, i.e., the null class), since the former has one member and the latter has no members, so we can identify the number 1 with this class (the class of things that are identical with 0). We now have two objects, and can then form the concept "is identical with 0 or 1" (using, in this case, the additional logical concept of disjunction). This gives us a corresponding class which we can identify with the number 2, and so on. Starting with the null class, then, and using only logical concepts, we can define all the natural numbers.

Can there be a set of all objects?

Introducing the idea of a class—or set or extension of a concept—offers us a new approach to our original question: how many things are there? If this question has an answer, then must there not be a class of all things? Leaving aside concepts, let us restrict ourselves to objects, taken as including logical objects such as classes or sets. Let us also switch here to talk of 'sets' rather than 'classes'. (For most purposes, you can think of the two terms as synonymous. Set theorists now draw a distinction between sets and classes, but we can ignore that here. 'Set' is used in what we are now going to discuss.) Is there a set of all objects? Obviously, if sets are themselves objects, then this set will contain itself, but is there any problem with this? To answer this, we need to introduce the idea of a *subset*, and to appreciate the relationship between a set and its subsets.

Consider a set of two objects, which we can write as '{a, b}', the curly brackets indicating that we have a set, with 'a' and 'b' standing for the two members of this set. How many subsets does this set have? By convention, both the null set—written as 'Ø'—and the set itself, in this case $\{a, b\}$, count as a subset of any set. This means that the answer is four: $\varnothing$, $\{a\}$, $\{b\}$, $\{a, b\}$. (You can think of a subset as representing a selection from the set. Suppose you are offered two cakes. You could take one or other (but not both) of them (if you are polite): that is two possible selections. But you could also take neither of them (if you are on a diet) or both of them (if you are especially hungry). So there are four possible selections in all.)

Similarly, a set of three objects, $\{a, b, c\}$, has eight subsets: $\varnothing$, $\{a\}$, $\{b\}$, $\{c\}$, $\{a, b\}$, $\{a, c\}$, $\{b, c\}$, $\{a, b, c\}$. In general, a set that has n members has 2^n subsets. But 2^n is always greater than n, which means that there are always more subsets than members of a set. (Each member alone forms a subset, and more subsets can be formed from combinations.) Consider, then, the set of all objects, i.e., the set whose members are all the objects there are. If sets, including subsets, are themselves objects, then there turn out to be more objects (viz. subsets) than there are objects (viz. members). Starting from the set of all objects, then, it seems that we can generate an even bigger set, the set of all its subsets, its so-called 'power set'. Since this is a contradiction (there cannot be more objects than there are objects), there can be no such set as the set of all objects. This form of argument is called *reductio ad absurdum* ('reduction to absurdity'): if a contradiction can be derived from a given hypothesis, then that gives us a reason to reject the hypothesis.

We thus have another way of saying what is wrong with the question 'How many things are there?' Even if we just mean by 'things' objects (as opposed to concepts), then it looks as if we cannot answer this question, certainly if sets are themselves objects. As soon as we collect together all objects (into a set) to count them, we can generate even more objects (by taking the set's subsets). One response, of course, is to reject the assumption that sets are objects. We will return to this in Chapter 2. But if we do reject it, then is it all right to form the set of all objects (i.e., to collect together all objects into a single set)? And if so, then can we answer the question of how many objects there are? Can we not just count them? But what is involved here? How do we count? What if the set is so large that we cannot, in practice, count all its members? What if it is so large, for example, that we would die before we could ever finish counting?

Infinity

At this point it might seem that the answer to the question 'How many things are there?' is obvious. Indeed, have we not missed the obvious answer right from the beginning? Can we not simply say 'infinity' or 'infinitely many'? Given that there are indefinitely many ways of thinking of things (through concepts), is this not the only possible answer? If just one thing (as it were) can be counted as one book, or 150 pages, or 38,000 words, or some even larger number of atoms, then should we not simply say that there is an 'infinite' number of things and be done with it?

'Infinity' is a word that is readily abused. As an answer to a question of how many, it can offer a quick way of *evading* the question—comparable to saying 'Somewhere else' in answering the question 'Where was I before I was conceived?' Such responses really just serve to cover up our embarrassment at not knowing how to answer the question properly. Sometimes, of course, 'infinity' is simply used to mean 'very large'—so large that one cannot, in fact, count the relevant things. We might call this its loose sense. But it also has a stricter sense which someone may intend in saying that there is an 'infinite' number of things.

Consider the set of natural numbers: $\{0, 1, 2, 3, 4, 5, \ldots\}$. Here we do indeed say that there is an *infinity* of such numbers. The series of natural numbers can be indefinitely extended: for any number in the series, the next one can be generated by adding 1, a process that can go on ad infinitum, as it is often put. This gives us a definite model for using the term 'infinity' in its strict sense. To say that a set has an infinite number of members is to say that it has the same number of members as the set of natural numbers.

But how do we judge sameness of number—i.e., that two sets have the same number of members? In the case of relatively small finite sets, we can just count the members and see if we get the same result. But in the case of relatively large finite or infinite sets, we cannot just count the members. So how can we compare them? Consider what is now called 'Galileo's Paradox' (Box 1). What answer would you give?

Box 1. Galileo's Paradox

Compare the following two sets, the set of natural numbers and the set of square numbers:

{0, 1, 2, 3, 4, 5, ...}

{0, 1, 4, 9, 16, 25, ...}

Which set is bigger, or do they have the same number of members? On the one hand, the first seems bigger because it includes all those numbers in the second *and more*. On the other hand, for every member of the first set there is a corresponding member of the second set, and vice versa, so surely they have the same number of members?

Our 'intuitions' about what to say here seem to conflict. What is happening is that we have *two* criteria for sameness of number that in the case of infinite sets come apart. On one criterion, two sets have the same number if neither is bigger than the other, in the sense of 'bigger than' for which a set is always bigger than any proper subset of itself (where talk of 'proper' excludes the case where the subset is the set itself). On the other criterion, two sets have the same number if their members can be correlated one–one with each other. In finite cases these two criteria give the same result. Consider, for example, the set of natural numbers up to (and including) 25 and the set of square numbers up to (and including) 25. Clearly the first is bigger than the second: the latter is a proper subset of the former. Nor can the two sets be one–one correlated. So the two sets do not have the same number of members.

In the case of infinite sets, however, the two criteria come apart. The set of square numbers is a proper subset of the set of natural numbers, yet the members of the two sets can be one–one correlated. So we clearly need to decide which of these two criteria is the key one. If we adopt the first, then it immediately follows that infinite sets come in many different sizes. But then how exactly are we to go about ordering them in size? It seems much simpler to adopt the second criterion. On this view, the two sets we have just considered do indeed have the same number of members because those members can be one–one correlated.

If this second criterion is adopted, then it would seem to give us a possible answer to our question of how many things there are. There is an 'infinite' number of things, where this means that there is the same number of things as there are natural numbers. This view allows, however, that the set of things may be either 'bigger' or 'smaller' than the set of natural numbers, in the sense of the first criterion. So are we still any further forward?

Beyond infinity

We have considered the set of natural numbers and found— counter-intuitively, perhaps—that this set has the same number of members as the set of square numbers, even though this latter set is in a sense 'smaller'. But are there 'bigger' sets than the set of natural numbers, in the sense of there being a set of which the set of natural numbers is a proper subset? The answer, of course, is yes. One example is the set of positive rational numbers, i.e., the set of numbers of the form p/q where p and q are natural numbers (excluding $q = 0$). This includes not only all the natural numbers but all the positive fractional numbers as well, such as ½, 1¼, 2¾, etc. So it is clearly 'bigger'. Indeed, it might seem 'infinitely' bigger, since between any two natural numbers there are infinitely many fractions, and this is repeated an infinite number of times. So we might think that what we have here is infinity × infinity.

It can be shown, however, that the set of natural numbers and the set of positive rational numbers actually have the same number of members—in the sense that they can be one–one correlated. To demonstrate this, let us represent the positive rational numbers in a table (Figure 1).

1/1	1/2 →	1/3	1/4 →	1/5	1/6 →	1/7	1/8 →	...
2/1	2/2	2/3	2/4	2/5	2/6	2/7	2/8	...
3/1	3/2	3/3	3/4	3/5	3/6	3/7	3/8	...
4/1	4/2	4/3	4/4	4/5	4/6	4/7	4/8	...
5/1	5/2	5/3	5/4	5/5	5/6	5/7	5/8	...
6/1	6/2	6/3	6/4	6/5	6/6	6/7	6/8	...
7/1	7/2	7/3	7/4	7/5	7/6	7/7	7/8	...
8/1	8/2	8/3	8/4	8/5	8/6	8/7	8/8	...
⋮	⋮	⋮	⋮	⋮	⋮	⋮	⋮	⋱

1. **Correlating the natural numbers and the rational numbers.**

Assuming that this table can be extended ad infinitum, as the ellipses indicate, it should be clear that all the positive rational numbers can be represented in this way. Of course, in doing it this way, each rational number is represented more than once, since, e.g., 2/2 is equivalent to 1/1. All the subsequent occurrences of a rational number are marked in italics in Figure 1.

Now remember that two sets have the same number of members (on the preferred criterion) if the members of each set can be one–one correlated. So imagine going through the table in Figure 1 as directed by the arrows, counting as one does so: 1, 2, 3, 4, 5, etc. If one skips all the italicized numbers, then what we have here is a way of correlating all the positive rational numbers with the natural numbers. So the two sets do indeed have the same number of members. Ingenious—there are just as many rational numbers as natural numbers!

Now consider the set of real numbers. This set comprises both the rational numbers and the irrational numbers. Irrational numbers are numbers that cannot be expressed as fractions, such as $\sqrt{2}$, $\sqrt{3}$, and π. Does the set of real numbers have the same number of members as the set of natural numbers? By this point you may well have no idea at all what to say: what 'intuitions' you might have had about such matters have already been shown to be shaky. This set is surely much, much bigger; and yet so was the set of rational numbers.

In fact, it can be demonstrated that the set of real numbers is 'genuinely' bigger than the set of natural numbers, even by the criterion of one–one correlation. To show this, let us assume as a hypothesis that the two sets *can* be one–one correlated and see if we can derive a contradiction from this hypothesis. Imagine, too, that the real numbers are expressed in decimal notation. It does not matter how we order the real numbers, as long as we pair a different real number with each natural number. So imagine the two sets can be correlated in the following way:

1. 1.000000000...
2. 1.333333333...
3. 3.141592653...
4. 9.698502193...
5. 2.718281828...
6. 7.428571429...

...   ...

If our hypothesis is right, then every real number should be represented in this table, extending as it does to infinity. However, it is now easy to form a real number that is *not* listed in the second column. One way to do so is to take the first digit in the first row and add one ($1 \rightarrow 2$), the second digit in the second row and add one ($3 \rightarrow 4$), the third digit in the third row and add one ($4 \rightarrow 5$), and so on, generating in this case the number 2.45938.... This number clearly differs from every number on this list in at least one decimal place. We can think of this number as being produced by taking a *diagonal* line through the second column of the table, and there are clearly indefinitely many such diagonal lines that can be taken, each of which can produce a real number not on the list. So the hypothesis that the set of real numbers can be one–one correlated with the set of natural numbers is false: there are *more* real numbers than there are natural numbers. Another way to put this is to say that the real numbers are *non-denumerable*, in other words, they cannot be counted.

This proof is no less ingenious than the previous one. It is now called Cantor's diagonal argument, after the German mathematician Georg Cantor (1845–1918), who first presented it in 1891. Its result is really quite remarkable: there is indeed more than one size of infinity! These 'infinities' were termed by Cantor *transfinite numbers*. The first transfinite number is called 'aleph-zero' (aleph being the first letter of the Hebrew alphabet) and written as '$\aleph_0$'. This is the number that answers the question: How many natural numbers are there? The next transfinite number is aleph-one, written as '$\aleph_1$'. This is the number that answers the question: how many real numbers are there?

Beginning with '$\aleph_0$' and '$\aleph_1$', Cantor showed how to generate a whole series of transfinite numbers, each one bigger than the previous one. We started with the thought that there is just one 'infinity'; if Cantor is right, then there is an 'infinity of infinities'—or more precisely, $\aleph_0$ transfinite numbers. The details here are more complicated, so we will end our thought-thinking trip through infinity at this point. The message to take home is that by seeking to clarify our ordinary notion of infinity, we can arrive at the more precise notion of the transfinite.

So how many things are there?

We thought we had an easy answer to the question of how many things there are: infinity. But we now see that this notion has many senses. Even if we ignore its loose sense, there are indefinitely many strict senses we can identify, from the first transfinite number, $\aleph_0$, onwards. So now we really don't know what to say in answer to our question. Even if there is an 'infinity' of things, is it $\aleph_0$ or $\aleph_1$ or some even larger number? If it is $\aleph_0$, then we can count those things, but if it is larger, then we cannot. If the natural numbers are themselves 'things', then, at the very least, there are $\aleph_0$ things, but if sets are 'things' as well, then not only are there far more than this but we are not even sure what answer could possibly be given. We have come a long way!

We started off with an apparently simple question and have ended up with some remarkable results. As a response to that question, however, our journey is just a long way of saying that we really do need to specify what *kind of thing* we have in mind in asking the question. If we mean natural numbers, then we can give a definite answer: $\aleph_0$. If we mean real numbers, then we can also give a definite (but different) answer: $\aleph_1$. If we mean some particular kind of ordinary finite objects, such as books or chairs or cells, then we may have to count them or find some appropriate way of working out or estimating how many. The simple question 'How many things are there?' does not permit a simple answer without specification of the relevant concept(s) by means of which to think of the things.

As suggested in the Introduction, this question is just one example of a typical philosophical question. Such questions may not have a straightforward answer, but in attempting to answer them or to show why they cannot be answered straightforwardly or are even 'meaningless', we have to undertake *analysis*—where this means, first and foremost, identifying their possible meanings and, if necessary, introducing new concepts to make those meanings more precise. It is often easy to give simple answers such as 'infinity', but when we analyse such terms, we tend to find that the issues are far more complex than they initially seemed. We may have to get clear about a whole host of other matters and may need to invent new terms, such as 'transfinite number', '$\aleph_0$', and so on, to do so. This is what makes analysis challenging and yet also both exciting and fruitful. It is not a simple matter of 'disentangling' or 'distinguishing'. Conceptual creativity is required to introduce appropriate concepts, which open up new forms and possibilities of thinking.

The kind of analysis illustrated in this chapter is indeed what inspired—and continues to inspire—the development of 'analytic' philosophy. We have looked here at concepts such as those of "thing", "object", "concept", "set", "number", and "infinity". But there are other important concepts, such as those of "existence", "meaning", "sense", "thought", "God", and "goodness", not to mention "analysis" itself, the elucidation of which also requires analysis. Some of these concepts will be explored in the chapters that follow. We will see further illustration of the conceptual creativity that lies at the heart of fruitful analysis.

Chapter 2
How can we speak of what does not exist?

If I tell you that I am a philosopher, how do you understand what I am saying? The most obvious account is that you know to whom 'I' (as used by me) refers, you know what it is to be a philosopher, and you understand that I am claiming that what it is to be a philosopher applies to me. In Frege's terminology (as introduced in Chapter 1), you understand that I am asserting that the object that is me falls under the concept "philosopher". Moreover, you know that my claim is true if I am indeed a philosopher—if I do indeed fall under the concept "philosopher".

If I tell you that my wife is a philosopher, how do you understand what I am saying? If you know who my wife is, then the account will be similar—you understand that I am asserting that this person falls under the concept "philosopher". But what if you do not know who she is? Here a different account would seem to be needed. One suggestion might be that you understand me to be claiming both that I have a wife and that she is a philosopher. To judge that this is true, you would then need to establish that both claims are true. But would you need to know who my wife is in order to (properly) understand my assertion, or would it be enough just to know that I am claiming to have a wife?

If I tell you that the King of France is a philosopher, how do you understand what I am saying? If you know that France no longer has a monarchy, then you may be at a loss to understand what I am saying, even though the words themselves make sense. Am I using the definite description 'the King of France' in some unusual way, or am I simply confused? And if I am apparently being serious, would you say that what I am saying is *false*? This is trickier, as saying it is false might be taken to imply that the King of France is not a philosopher, but has some other occupation.

If I tell you that Pangloss is a philosopher, how do you understand what I am saying? If you know Voltaire's novel *Candide*, then you will know that Pangloss is a fictional character (albeit one based on the actual philosopher Leibniz). But is my claim therefore true if Pangloss is indeed a philosopher in this novel? Some philosophers (such as Frege) have argued that statements about fictional objects cannot be true but should instead be regarded as neither true nor false. Whatever one says about the truth-value of a fictional statement, however, it does seem that what you need to know in order to understand such a statement is different from what you need to know in the first three cases we have considered. To know what 'Pangloss' means, we need to identify the work of fiction in which this name is used.

These four cases, simple examples of asserting that someone is a philosopher, already suggest that there is no straightforward general account of how we understand even such simple statements. Statements that purportedly refer to something that does not exist, whether fictional or not, have been especially problematic in the history of philosophy. If I claim that I can draw an icosahedron, then there is something that I am claiming to be able to draw: a geometrical solid figure with twenty faces (of which there are various kinds). But if I claim that no one can draw a square circle, then I am not claiming that there is something that they cannot draw, just because there is nothing that could be such a thing. Or am I? Can we refer to 'impossible things'? There is clearly a need for analysis here—to help us understand what is really going on when we speak of what does not exist.

Existential statements

What is it to claim that something does or does not exist? Is this like claiming that someone is or is not a philosopher? In the latter case, this would be to claim—in Frege's terminology—that a particular object falls under the (first-level) concept "philosopher". So is to claim that something exists to claim that a particular object falls under the (first-level) concept "exists"? This does not seem right: if these concepts represent properties, then the property of existence seems to be a different kind of property to the property of being a philosopher. The problem is perhaps most obvious if we consider negative existential statements, such as the (true) statement that unicorns do not exist. What is it that is being said not to exist? Don't unicorns have to exist in some sense to say anything whatever about them? Some philosophers have suggested that we need to distinguish between 'existence' and 'subsistence'. Unicorns may not exist (in the actual, spatio-temporal world) but they must somehow subsist (in some 'ideal' world) to be able to talk about them.

Talk of 'subsistence' seems too quick a fix to the problem that negative existential statements raise—comparable to just saying 'infinity' to the question of how many things there are in the world that was discussed in Chapter 1. From what was said in that chapter, however, we have the resources to solve the problem in a more satisfying way. In particular, we need to recall Frege's claim that number statements are assertions about concepts. Existential statements need to be understood in exactly the same way. Indeed, they are really just a type of number statement, since to say that unicorns do not exist is to say that there are no instances of unicorns, in other words, that the concept "unicorn" has 0 instances.

It was mentioned in Chapter 1 that Frege was the founder of modern logic. His crucial innovation was the invention of a notation for *quantifier phrases*, phrases which say *how many* of something there are. Two of the most important are phrases of the form 'all *As*' and 'some *As*', used in saying, for example, that all philosophers are human or that some philosophers are logicians. The first is symbolized using the so-called universal quantifier, written as an upside-down A: ∀. The second is symbolized using the existential quantifier, written as a backwards E: ∃. (Frege did not invent these particular symbols, but they are used now instead of his own, slightly more complex symbolism. The idea is the same.) The first will be illustrated later on in this chapter. The second is relevant here, as it is needed in formalizing existential statements.

In modern (quantificational) logic, the statement that unicorns do not exist is formalized as follows:

$$\neg(\exists x)Ux.$$

This can be read as 'It is not the case that there is some x such that x is a U', where '¬' is the sign for negation, '$\exists x$' represents 'there is some x (such that ...)', using the existential quantifier, and 'Ux' abbreviates 'x is a U', with 'U' symbolizing the concept "unicorn". More simply, this might be read as 'It is not the case that there are some unicorns'. Here what is crucial is the difference between 'Ux' and '$(\exists x)\,Ux$'. 'Ux' symbolizes the case of an object x falling under the first-level concept "U", '$(\exists x)\,Ux$' symbolizes the case of the first-level concept "U" falling within the second-level concept "is instantiated". To say that a concept is instantiated is to say that there is something (at least one thing) that falls under it, but this is a property that the concept has. It is not to say *which* object or objects fall under it, which is what we are indeed saying when we say, for example, that I am a philosopher.

When we make an existential claim, then, we are not attributing a first-level concept to an object, but a second-level concept to a first-level concept. We do not then need to suppose that unicorns must somehow 'subsist' to say anything about them at all, even when what we are saying is that they do not exist. When we say that unicorns do not exist, we are not talking about unicorns but about the *concept* of being a unicorn: we are saying that this concept is not instantiated, that is, has no instances. Frege's logical analysis, then, offers a nice resolution of the problem raised by negative existential statements. Just like number statements generally, existential statements (whether positive or negative) are assertions about concepts.

Does a perfect God exist?

One of the most famous arguments in the history of philosophy is the so-called ontological argument for the existence of God. (Ontology is the study of being, concerned with what things, and kinds of things, exist, and in what ways.) In its simplest form, this can be set out as follows:

Analytic Philosophy

(1) God has every perfection (i.e., every perfect property).

(2) Existence is a perfection.

Therefore: (3) God exists.

This argument is clearly valid: if the premises are true, then the conclusion must be true. But is the argument *sound*—in other words, does it have true premises in addition to being valid? All the first premise says is that God is the most perfect being—something that we might think is true simply by definition. What about the second premise? Is it not more perfect to exist than not to exist? Perhaps properties such as benevolence, omniscience, and omnipotence can be regarded as perfections, but can existence be regarded as a perfection?

The ontological argument, as presented here, looks far too quick to be sound. Can we really draw an ontological conclusion, concerning what exists, from what look like mere definitional claims? Are we not just building existence into our definition of God? By a similar argument, could we not prove the existence of the devil? Here is how the argument might go:

(4)   The devil has every scary property.

(5)   Existence is a scary property.

Therefore: (6)   The devil exists.

The devil is the scariest thing there could be, right? But surely a devil that exists is far more scary than one that does not. Who would be scared of a non-existent devil (Figure 2)?

2. The scariest devil?

This devilish analogue should confirm one's suspicions of the ontological argument for the existence of God. If Frege's view of existential statements is correct, however, then we have a neat diagnosis of what is wrong here: it is treating existence as a first-level property whereas it should really be regarded as a second-level property. Or more accurately, existential claims should be understood in terms of the instantiation of concepts. To say that God exists, on this view, is to say that the concept "God" is (uniquely) instantiated. We can define the (first-level) concept of God as containing other (first-level) concepts such as those of being benevolent, omniscient, and omnipotent, but this does not entitle us to draw any conclusion as to whether such a concept is instantiated. We can accept premise (1) of the argument, in other words, but premise (2) is false, if by 'perfection' we mean a first-level property. (If we mean anything else, then the argument is no longer valid.)

Needless to say, more sophisticated versions of the ontological argument have been developed over the centuries, and the argument continues to generate controversy today. Justice cannot be done to this here; the key point is just to illustrate the philosophical work that can be done in accepting Frege's analysis of number and existential statements as assertions about concepts and the related distinction between first-level and second-level concepts.

Introducing Bertrand Russell

Bertrand Russell (1872–1970) is one of the intellectual giants of the 20th century. Not only is he one of the founders of analytic philosophy but he was also active in politics, and wrote on a wide range of social and ethical issues. He was born in Wales and studied mathematics and then philosophy at Cambridge, where he was elected to a Fellowship in 1896 on the basis of a dissertation on the foundations of geometry. After initially being attracted to British idealism, the philosophical tradition that was then dominant in Britain, he rejected it on the grounds that it could not do justice to mathematics, and he then devoted himself, like Frege, to showing that arithmetic (and geometry, too, in Russell's case) could be reduced to logic. Russell's logicist views were first presented in *The Principles of Mathematics*, published in 1903, and those views were revised and a detailed formal demonstration offered in his main work, *Principia Mathematica*, published in three volumes between 1910 and 1913. This work was written with his former mathematics teacher at Cambridge, A. N. Whitehead (1861–1947), who was to become a significant philosopher in his own right.

Like Frege, Russell defined the natural numbers as classes, using only logical concepts. Unlike Frege, however, he came to believe that classes should not be taken as objects, whether logical or not. Rather, he argued, they are 'logical fictions'. In the remainder of this chapter we will see how Russell came to hold this view and how he thought that we could nevertheless talk about such fictions. Central to his answer was his theory of descriptions, which was first presented in a paper called 'On Denoting' in 1905 and which has ever since been regarded as a paradigm of analysis. To understand what motivated it, we need to go back to the definition of numbers as classes.

Russell's paradox

In Chapter 1 we considered the paradox that arises when we take the set of all things and regard the subsets of a set as themselves things: we can generate an even bigger set, its power set. It was this paradox that led Russell to discover a further paradox, which is now named after him: *Russell's paradox*. Russell himself formulated the paradox in terms of 'classes' rather than 'sets', so let us follow him in discussing it in these terms (Box 2).

Box 2. Russell's paradox

Consider the class of horses. This class is not itself a horse, so the class is not a member of itself. Consider the class of non-horses. This class is not a horse, so the class *is* a member of itself. So some classes are members of themselves and some classes are not members of themselves. Consider now the class of all classes that are not members of themselves. Is this a member of itself or not? If it is, then since it is the class of all classes that are not members of themselves, it is not. If it is not, then since this is the defining property of the classes it contains, it is. We have a contradiction.

Why should this contradiction trouble us? Why should we not just deny that there can be any such class as the class of classes that are not members of themselves, just as one would deny that there is any such set as the set of all things? The problem is that the defining condition for such a class seems perfectly logical. If we allow the concepts of a class and of class-membership, then we can legitimately form the concepts of a class being a member of itself and of a class not being a member of itself. The concept of a class being a member of itself seems to determine a legitimate class: the class of classes that are members of themselves. (Is this class a member of itself or not? If it is, then it is; and if is not, then it is not; so no contradiction arises here.) So the concept of a class not being a member of itself ought also to determine a legitimate class: the class of classes that are not members of themselves. Yet it is the idea of this class that generates a contradiction.

In Chapter 1, I mentioned the principle that for every concept there is a class of things that fall under it. There can be such a class even when the defining concept is logically contradictory (such as the concept of not being identical with itself): in this case the class is the null class. But the class of classes that are not members of themselves cannot be the null class, because it has members: all the classes that are not members of themselves (such as the class of horses). In fact, what we seem to have here is a defining concept that is logically legitimate but a corresponding class that cannot exist because it has logically contradictory properties (it both is and is not a member of itself). So the principle that for every concept there is a class of things that fall under it seems to be false. Russell's paradox shows that there is at least one counter-example.

Compare this with the concept of a square circle. There can be no such *object* as a square circle because nothing can have contradictory properties. But there is indeed a corresponding class, in this case the null class. However, this is different from what we have in the case of Russell's paradox. It is the class (of classes that are not members of themselves) that is contradictory: there can be no such object as this class. And yet if the defining concept for this class is logically legitimate, then there ought to be such a class, if the principle that for every concept there is a class of things that fall under it were true. We have an example of a term that seems to be perfectly meaningful—'the class of classes that are not members of themselves'—but which (demonstrably) fails to refer.

Given that both Frege and Russell wanted to define numbers in terms of classes (and indeed, classes of classes), determined by logically legitimate concepts, Russell's paradox is potentially devastating. Russell wrote to Frege in June 1902 informing him of the contradiction he had discovered, and Frege immediately recognized its significance, replying that it threatened the very foundations that he had hoped to establish for arithmetic. At the time that Frege received Russell's letter, the second volume of Frege's main work, *Basic Laws of Arithmetic*, was in press, the first volume having been published in 1893. In this work Frege attempted to demonstrate, formally, what he had sketched, informally, in *The Foundations of Arithmetic* of 1884, the book whose central idea (that number statements are assertions about concepts) was explained in Chapter 1. Frege attempted to respond to Russell's paradox in a hastily written appendix to the second volume of *Basic Laws*. But he soon realized that this response was inadequate, and ended up abandoning his logicist project, devoting the rest of his life to the clarification of his logical ideas. Russell did not give up so easily, however, and devoted the next ten years of his life to solving the paradox and attempting to show how the logicist project could nevertheless be carried out. As we will see in Chapter 4, Russell's paradox is also what drew Wittgenstein into philosophy. Given its centrality to the development of analytic philosophy, let us look in more detail at how it arises and what responses are available.

Responding to Russell's paradox

Russell's paradox arises from attempting to form a class determined by the concept "is a class that is not a member of itself". If there is such a class, then we ought to be able to ask whether this class falls under its determining concept or not. If it does, then it does not, and if it does not, then it does; so we have our contradiction. One response is to deny that there is such a class; but this violates the principle that for every concept there is a class of things that fall under it. A second response is to simply exclude the case of a class falling under its determining concept.

This second response was essentially Frege's response. Classes cannot be taken to fall under their determining concepts. One problem with this is that it does not prevent related paradoxes from arising. More importantly, it fails to explain *why* a class cannot fall under its determining concept. Merely excluding this case because it generates a contradiction seems ad hoc: it provides no principled reason for the exclusion. It is not surprising that Frege soon gave up his logicist project.

Russell's response was more radical and offered a philosophical rationale. On his account, we can legitimately talk about classes but they should be seen as 'logical fictions' rather than objects, properly speaking. As such, no class can fall under its determining concept. Every concept does indeed determine a class, but this class is not something of which it can be asked whether it falls under its determining concept or not. So the paradox cannot arise.

Russell's response was embedded in a theory—his so-called theory of types—that was intended to provide a philosophical justification of his solution to the paradox. On this theory, there is a *hierarchy* of objects and classes. At the most basic level, there are 'genuine' objects—objects such as books, chairs, horses, and so on. At the next level, there are classes of objects—such as the class of horses and the class of non-horses (which contains all those genuine objects, such as books and chairs, that are not horses). Then there are classes of classes of objects, and so on up the hierarchy. The key point is that something at any given level can only be a member of a class at a higher level. This automatically rules out any class being a member of itself; so no contradiction can be generated.

We have already met the idea of a hierarchy in discussing Frege's views in Chapter 1: there are first-level concepts, second-level concepts, and so on. What Russell is saying is that there is not just a hierarchy of concepts but also a hierarchy of objects—genuine objects, (first-level) classes of objects, (second-level) classes of classes of objects, and so on. First-level classes can be members of second-level classes but cannot be members of other first-level classes, just as first-level concepts can fall within second-level concepts but not other first-level concepts. So what is ruled out is not just a class being a member of itself (which is what generates the contradiction) but any class being a member of a class that is not of a higher level. Russell offers a more general theory from which a solution to the paradox is derived.

According to Russell, then, there are different *types* of things, and what can be said about things of one type cannot necessarily be said about things of some other type. Indeed, the attempt to say, for example, that a class is or is not a member of itself results in nonsense. We will explore this idea further in Chapter 4, in discussing its significance for Wittgenstein. Here, however, we need to say more about the idea of classes as logical fictions.

Do average people exist?

According to Russell, the only genuine objects are those at the base of the hierarchy. Classes are 'logical fictions'. If classes are not genuine objects, then the problem of any of them having contradictory properties evaporates. However, like Frege, Russell still wants to argue that numbers are classes. But if numbers, too, are therefore logical fictions, then does this not mean that numbers do not exist? This was not Frege's view. According to Frege, numbers had to exist in order for true statements about them to be made. So what does it mean for something to be a 'logical fiction'? And how does this still enable us to say true things about them?

Let us go back to the kind of simple statement with which we began this chapter. I tell you that my wife has three children. Here you understand what I am saying by knowing who my wife is (or grasping my claim to have a wife), knowing what it is to have three children, and understanding that I am claiming that what it is to have three children applies to my wife. My statement is true if I do indeed have a wife and she has three children. But now consider the following claim:

(A1)   The average British woman has 1.9 children.

Here there is no such person as the average British woman, and even if there were, she could not have 1.9 children! So what is it you understand in grasping this claim, and what is it for it to be true (or false, as the case may be)? What we mean might be expressed as follows:

(A2)   The total number of children of British women divided by the total number of British women equals 1.9.

This makes clear what we need to know to work out whether the claim is true. We need to know how many British women there are, as well as how many children each of them has. In this case we need to know something about *every* British woman, not just one woman.

The claim that the average British woman has 1.9 children, then, is really just a disguised claim about all British women. (A1) offers us a useful abbreviation of (A2), enabling us to compare more easily the situation in different countries, for example. We can say such things as 'While the average British woman has 1.9 children, the average Chinese woman has 1.5 children'. 'The average British woman' and 'the average Chinese woman' are *logical fictions*. No such women exist, but the terms provide a convenient way of talking, enabling us to make true statements more simply.

Talk of classes can be analysed in a similar way. One example will suffice here. Consider the following statement:

(C1)   The class of horses is a subclass of the class of animals.

Do we need to suppose that such classes 'exist' in order for this statement to be true? Not at all, on Russell's view. What (C1) 'really means' might be expressed as follows:

(C2)   Anything that falls under the concept "horse" falls under the concept "animal".

This is a claim about concepts, not classes. In modern (quantificational) logic, it would be symbolized as follows:

(C3) $(\forall x)(Hx \rightarrow Ax)$.

This can be read as 'For all x, if x is a horse, then x is an animal', where '$\forall x$' represents 'for all x', using the universal quantifier, 'Hx' abbreviates 'x is a H', with 'H' symbolizing the concept "horse", 'Ax' abbreviates 'x is an A', with 'A' symbolizing the concept "animal", and '$\rightarrow$' represents 'if…then…'. This makes clear that the statement concerns a relationship between two concepts—that if anything instantiates the first concept, then it also instantiates the second. We need only to suppose that concepts 'exist', not classes as well.

Given the close connection between classes and concepts, as captured in the principle that for every concept there is a class determined by it, talk of classes can always be translated into talk of their corresponding concepts. Concepts are 'ontologically prior' to the classes they determine, as philosophers would say. It is this idea that lies behind Russell's claim that classes are logical fictions—or, as he also puts it, 'logical constructions'. Talk of classes is 'constructed' out of our talk of concepts, in a similar way to how talk of 'the average woman' is constructed out of our talk of actual women.

According to Frege and Russell, (C2), and its formalization as (C3), also expresses what is 'really meant' by the following, more ordinary statement:

(C4)   All horses are animals.

This, too, is understood as saying that if anything is a horse, then it is an animal, making clear that the statement is about concepts. (C1), (C2), (C3), and (C4) are thus all seen as saying the same thing, but (C2) makes clearest what is going on, logically speaking, with (C3) its logical formalization. We shall explore the issue of what statements 'really mean' in much more detail in Chapters 3 and 4. Before doing so, however, we need to introduce Russell's most famous theory, the theory of descriptions.

The theory of descriptions

Let us once again go back to the kind of simple statements with which we began this chapter. If I tell you that Bertrand is a philosopher, then you understand what I am saying by knowing what the name 'Bertrand' refers to, grasping the concept "philosopher", and recognizing that I am claiming that that concept applies to Bertrand. But now consider the following statement:

(K1)   The King of France is a philosopher.

(I am adapting one of Russell's own examples here, which was 'The present King of France is bald'.) Here what we have is not a name, such as 'Bertrand', but a definite description, a phrase of the form 'the *F*'. How do I understand this statement, given that France is no longer a monarchy and no King of France exists, in other words, that the definite description 'the King of France' does not refer to anything?

By now we should know what answer to expect. The statement needs to be analysed to make clear that what is 'really involved' is an assertion about concepts. According to Russell, what (K1) 'really means' is the following:

 (K2) There is one and only one King of France, and whatever is King of France is a philosopher.

We can regard this as a conjunction of three simpler statements, each of which is about the concept "King of France":

 (K2a) There is at least one King of France.
 (K2b) There is at most one King of France.
 (K2c) Whatever is King of France is a philosopher.

The first asserts that the concept "King of France" is instantiated, which we have already seen would be formalized using the existential quantifier as '$(\exists x)\, Kx$', with 'K' representing the concept "King of France". The third we are now also in a position to understand and formalize. It is similar to (C4) above, the statement that all horses are animals, which was formalized as (C3). So (K2c) would be formalized as '$(\forall x)\, (Kx \rightarrow Px)$', with '$P$' representing the concept "philosopher". The second is a little trickier. It asserts that the concept "King of France" does not have more than one instance. Logicians formalize this as:

$$(\forall x)(\forall y)(Kx\ \&\ Ky \rightarrow y = x).$$

What this literally says is that for all x and for all y, if x is King of France and y is King of France, then y is identical to x. This amounts to saying that there is not, in fact, more than one thing that is King of France (there could be none).

Putting these three formalizations together, and simplifying, we have the following formalization of (K2):

(K3) $\quad (\exists x)\big(Kx \,\&\, (\forall y)(Ky \to y = x)\,\&\, Px\big).$

This can be read as 'There is an x (at least one x) such that x is K, and for any y such that y is K, then y is identical with x, and x is P'. More succinctly, it can be read as:

(K4) There is one and only one K and that thing is P.

To understand the original statement (K1), then, requires only that we understand the concepts "King of France" and "philosopher", as well as all the relevant logical concepts, in this case those of existential and universal quantification (represented using '$\exists$' and '$\forall$'), conjunction ('$\&$'), the 'if…then' conditional ('$\to$'), and identity ('$=$'). We do not need to know what 'the King of France' means, in the sense of knowing to whom the phrase refers. Indeed, according to Russell, this phrase has no meaning at all, precisely because there is no King of France. But that does not stop the statement as a whole having a meaning, or us from understanding the statement, because it is not about the King of France but about the *concept* "King of France". On Russell's analysis, then, what the statement says might be better expressed as follows:

(K5) The concept "King of France" is uniquely instantiated and whatever instantiates this concept also instantiates the concept "philosopher".

If there is, in fact, no King of France, then the statement will come out false (because the constituent statement (K2a) is false: the concept "King of France" is not instantiated at all).

Since it was first introduced in 1905, Russell's theory of descriptions has both provided a model of analysis for subsequent analytic philosophers and generated a great deal of debate and controversy. We will discuss it further in the chapters that follow. There is also a lot that could be said about what motivated it. The problem of how we can speak of what does not exist was only one motivation. But it was one of the most important motivations, since its solution allowed Russell to hold that classes are logical fictions and hence to resolve the paradox that bears his name. The theory of descriptions showed, according to Russell, that a definite description could contribute to the meaning of a sentence in which it appears without having meaning in itself. Phrases such as 'the King of France' or 'the class of objects that are not self-identical' may not refer to anything, but we can still make meaningful statements (statements that are either true or false) by using them.

So how can we speak of what does not exist?

Frege's analysis of existential statements and Russell's theory of descriptions suggest that statements that purport to refer to non-existent objects should be understood as assertions about concepts. In saying (truly) that unicorns do not exist, for example, what I 'really mean' is that the concept "unicorn" is not instantiated, and in claiming (falsely, according to Russell) that the present King of France is a philosopher, what I 'really mean' is that the concept "King of France" is uniquely instantiated and that whatever falls under this concept also falls under the concept "philosopher". So I can speak of what does not exist by using appropriate concepts.

According to Russell, classes—and hence numbers—do not exist; they are logical fictions. But we can make sense of how we can nevertheless speak of them by analysing statements about them in an appropriate way, once again 'reducing' them to assertions about concepts. This strategy opens up the possibility of a general programme of analysis, 'reducing' as many statements as we can to some privileged core of statements. This strategy lay at the heart of what came to be called 'logical atomism', which Russell pursued together with Wittgenstein in the late 1910s, as we will see in Chapter 4.

Throughout this chapter, I have talked of statements being analysed into what they 'really mean', putting 'really mean' in scare quotes each time to signal that this is something that we need to explore further. We can make sense of how we can speak of what does not exist, it seems, only if we can translate statements that purport to refer to what does not exist into statements that make clear their 'real meaning'. It is now time to explore some of the issues raised by such talk of 'real meaning'.

Chapter 3
Do you know what I mean?

If an anthropologist from outer space were to come to Earth and listen in on our conversations, then they might be struck by the frequency with which we ask if the person we are talking to knows what we mean. We use many phrases in both spoken and written language that express uncertainty as to whether we have expressed ourselves properly, or that show recognition that we have not, or that seek for reassurance along the way as to whether we are being understood. Know what I mean? As well as 'know what I mean', such phrases include 'as it were', 'so to say', 'roughly speaking', 'as a first approximation', 'somehow', 'sort of', 'kind of', '*et cetera*', 'and so on', 'you know', and 'like'. (There are analogous phrases in many other languages, so the phenomenon is not restricted to the English-speaking world.) At a more sophisticated level, we also use a variety of analogies, diagrams, examples, illustrations, metaphors, and similes in an attempt to explain ourselves. We also have a range of expressions that attempt to describe this process and its intended result—'getting the message across', 'understanding the gist', 'grasping the point', 'catching the drift', and 'cottoning on', to mention just some.

From the very origins of philosophy (both Western and non-Western), philosophers have been especially conscious of the inadequacies and limitations of language. But they have disagreed on whether this reflects a corresponding deficiency in thought, on what its explanation and implications are, and on how we should respond—in short, on what this itself means.

In the conversations of everyday life, we may talk loosely and inaccurately, but given time, or if we think hard enough about something, are we not bound, sooner or later, to come up with the right way to express ourselves? How many times have you thought of the perfect response to someone's witticism or criticism, but only after the opportunity to give it has passed? And, in any case, do we not regularly re-express what someone has told us, whether to clarify what they have said or in telling someone else later? So are these not all cases in which there are clear thoughts to be grasped, the task just being to find the appropriate articulation?

On the other hand, how many times have you found someone else putting the point you were struggling to make so much more elegantly or succinctly than you could have done? And we have a variety of idioms, such as 'That's spot on' and 'You've hit the nail on the head', to express this common experience. Are these not cases where someone else not merely knows what I mean but knows *better* what I mean? But what does *this* mean? Does it mean, for example, that I did not really know what I meant in such cases? Yet, if I can indeed recognize that someone else has neatly articulated what I was trying to say, then must I not have known what I meant? If I had not already grasped the thought in some form, then how could I say that someone else has captured just that thought? I do not say, for example, 'That's a good thought you've just had', but 'That's precisely my thought—well put!'. Alexander Pope made the point, with poetic elegance and succinctness, in *An Essay on Criticism* over 300 years ago:

> True wit is nature to advantage dressed,
> What oft was thought, but ne'er so well expressed;
> Something whose truth convinced at sight we find,
> That gives us back the image of our mind.

The same questions can be raised concerning philosophical debate; indeed, they seem to arise in an even starker form, as our discussion in Chapters 1 and 2 illustrates. When I say that there are 'infinite' square numbers, for example, do I really know what I mean? If I become convinced that there are $\aleph_0$ such numbers, is that what I really meant? What do I mean when I say that unicorns do not exist? That the first-level concept of being a unicorn falls within the second-level concept of being not instantiated? Here there seems a stronger case for saying that this is what I meant than in the example of the number of square numbers. But in both cases I am being given new conceptual resources to express more accurately what it was I meant—or if not this, then maybe what it was I *should* have meant. And this is exactly what philosophical analysis is intended to achieve.

Interpretive analysis

What does 'analysis' mean? If asked today, many people would say that it involves breaking something down to reveal its constituent parts and structure. This is indeed an important sense of 'analysis', which we can call its 'decompositional' sense, but it is not the only sense. The word has its origins in the ancient Greek term '*analusis*', which first acquired a technical sense in Euclidean geometry, where it meant the process of working back to first principles or more basic figures by means of which something could then be proved or constructed—through a corresponding process of 'synthesis'. This can be called its 'regressive' sense, which we also find illustrated throughout the history of mathematics, philosophy, and science. When Frege and Russell sought to 'reduce' arithmetic to logic, for example, they were seeking the supposedly more fundamental principles of logic (axioms, definitions, and rules of inference) by means of which to prove the laws and theorems of arithmetic. This is regressive analysis.

There is a third sense of 'analysis', however, which is just as important as the first two, and which is especially characteristic of analytic philosophy. This is 'interpretive' analysis, and we have already seen it illustrated in Chapters 1 and 2. Frege's analysis of existential and number statements, for example, consists in *interpreting* them as assertions about concepts, and likewise, Russell's theory of descriptions *interprets* sentences involving definite descriptions as expressing claims about concepts. Based on these interpretive analyses, decompositional analysis can then be used to identify the constituent elements in each case, such as the relevant concepts, whether empirical (e.g., the first-level concept of a unicorn, which might in turn be 'decomposed' into the concepts of a horse and of a horn) or logical (e.g., the second-level concept of being instantiated). We can also see such analyses as having a regressive dimension, in that the aim is to work back to what are seen as the more basic elements (in these cases, the relevant concepts). So it should be stressed that in actual cases of analysis, all three dimensions—interpretive, decompositional and regressive—are typically involved.

The relationship between these three dimensions of analysis will be an important theme in the rest of the book, and we will draw together some of the threads in Chapter 6. But let us focus here on interpretive analysis and consider how this raises the questions we have just asked concerning meaning. Let us take Russell's interpretive analysis of 'The present King of France is a philosopher' as 'The concept "King of France" is uniquely instantiated and whatever instantiates this concept also instantiates the concept "philosopher"'. Is this what someone *means* when they understand the original sentence? If asked what that sentence means, most people are highly unlikely to give you the Russellian analysis: one needs acquaintance with the theory of descriptions (and the account given in Chapter 2) to rustle that up! But that is precisely the point. What interpretive analysis typically offers are richer conceptual resources to elucidate that meaning. It would be tempting to say that interpretive analysis tells us what something *really* means or what we *should* mean. But how we are to understand, explain, or even just describe all this? As we will see, the issues raised by interpretive analysis came to be addressed and explored by analytic philosophers themselves.

Introducing G. E. Moore

G. E. Moore (1873–1958) is generally regarded, alongside Russell, as having inaugurated analytic philosophy in Britain through their joint rebellion against British idealism at the turn of the 20th century. Indeed, Russell credits Moore with having made the first move, with him following close behind. Whereas Russell's main interests at the time lay in the philosophy of mathematics and logic, however, Moore's concern was with *epistemology* (the theory of knowledge) and ethics. Like Russell he was educated at Cambridge and was elected to a Fellowship, in Moore's case in 1898, two years after Russell. He left Cambridge when his Fellowship ended in 1904 but returned in 1911 to take up a lectureship in moral science. He was Professor from 1925 until he retired in 1939 (when Wittgenstein succeeded him), and was Editor of *Mind*, one of the top journals of philosophy, from 1921 to 1944. He spent most of the Second World War in the States, lecturing in New York and California, among other places, thereby encouraging the development of analytic philosophy in North America.

His most famous work was *Principia Ethica*, published in 1903, but he also published a number of influential papers, including 'A Defence of Common Sense' (1925) and 'Proof of an External World' (1939), aimed at refuting both idealism and scepticism. Moore made it his task to distinguish and clarify as carefully as he could the precise questions asked by philosophers and the various answers that might be given to these questions, without committing himself, in many cases, to any definitive answers. As a result, he can often come across as unduly pedantic in his writing, but he had an enormous influence on those he taught and with whom he engaged in philosophical discussion. What he bequeathed was more his analytic approach than any characteristic set of doctrines or ideas.

Can 'good' be defined'?

The central question of *Principia Ethica* is 'What is good?', and Moore's main claim is that 'good' is indefinable, or, as it might also be put, that goodness is unanalysable and hence has to be regarded as a simple quality. His main argument for this is the 'open question argument', as it has come to be called. Consider a possible definition of 'good', say, as 'that which we desire to desire', which Moore himself takes as one of the more plausible. It seems, though, that we can quite genuinely ask 'Is that which we desire to desire good?' This question seems *open* in a way that the question 'Is what is good good?' or 'Is that which we desire to desire that which we desire to desire?' is not. The answer to these last two questions is obviously 'yes', as we are simply being asked to agree to a tautology—to what is self-evidently true. Yet if 'good' (or 'what is good') and 'that which we desire to desire' had exactly the same meaning, then all of these questions should be equally closed. Since a similar argument could be run for *any* purported definition of 'good', then it would seem that 'good' must be taken as indefinable.

This argument is far too quick to be true; indeed, it threatens to rule out any definition of anything, not just of 'good', other than obvious tautologies. Yet there seem to be many examples of true definitions that are far from obvious tautologies. The standard example is 'Water is H_2O'. Can we not easily imagine situations in which the question 'Is water H_2O?' is *open* in a way in which 'Is water water?' is clearly not? For example, someone could know what water is, in the sense of knowing that it is something we drink, what is found in rivers and oceans, what comes out of taps, and so on, and they could also know what H_2O is, in the sense of knowing that it is a molecule formed of two hydrogen atoms and one oxygen atom. But they might not have put the two together. For them, the question as whether water is H_2O would be open: it would come as a *discovery* to learn what the scientific definition of 'water' is.

Why should the situation not be the same in ethics? As a 'moral scientist', should Moore not have been trying to discover the nature of goodness just as a chemist seeks to discover the nature of a particular substance? It is here we touch on one of the deepest problems of philosophy, and not just of analytic philosophy. Are ethical questions ones that can be answered by using the methods and results of natural science? Those who say 'yes' are called *naturalists*, and the debate between naturalism and non-naturalism is not just confined to ethics, but rages fiercely in many other areas of philosophy. Frege, for example, attacked all forms of naturalism in the philosophy of mathematics; one major motivation behind his attempt to show that arithmetic is basically logical was to repudiate empirical and psychological accounts of number.

Moore was convinced that naturalistic accounts of ethics were mistaken: they all commit what he called the 'naturalistic fallacy', as his open question argument was intended to demonstrate. Any attempt to define 'good' naturalistically, whether in terms of pleasure, happiness, desires, or whatever, falls foul of the open question argument. So how did he see the situation as different from natural science? Much has been written about this; but let me try to identify one of his underlying thoughts. In the case of an ethical question, such as in asking whether something is 'good' or a course of action 'right', we do not need to do any scientific investigation; we have the resources to answer the question ourselves. We will need to know all the relevant facts, of course, but these alone will not give us the answer; we must also apply our ethical concepts and beliefs, which we already have. In principle these are sufficient: we do not need to wait for natural science to supply the answer.

Moore spoke here of 'intuition', and this has also generated a great deal of controversy, but again the basic idea is simple. All we can do is put ourselves in a position (by considering all the facts) to see the simple quality that is called 'good' (if it is there) in the same way as we need to put ourselves in an appropriate position (in the right lighting conditions, etc.) to see what colour something is. It is in elaborating and defending some such account of how we apprehend supposedly non-natural qualities that is perhaps the biggest challenge to non-naturalism, while the biggest challenge to naturalism is in providing convincing definitions of 'good' and other ethical terms. The question of whether 'good' can be defined remains very much open today.

How can analyses be both correct and informative?

Moore's open question argument makes a key assumption: that if you understand the meanings of two phrases, then you can immediately tell whether those meanings are the same or not. You can understand the meaning of 'good' and 'that which we desire to desire', for example, and immediately tell, according to Moore, that they are different. But as noted above, this threatens *any* attempt to define or analyse something. Moore's assumption, in fact, generates what has since been called *the paradox of analysis* (Box 3). If analyses are what analytic philosophy essentially seeks to provide, then it would seem to be fatally flawed at its very core.

Box 3. The paradox of analysis

Consider an analysis of the form 'A is B', where 'A' represents what is analysed and 'B' what is offered as the analysis. Then either 'A' and 'B' have the same meaning, in which case the analysis expresses a trivial identity; or else they do not, in which case the analysis is incorrect. So no analysis can be both correct and informative.

One might accept that some definitions are indeed uninformative. Consider the definition of '2' as '1 + 1' or that of 'puppy' as 'young dog'. Can anyone understand the various terms here and not immediately know that '2' and '1 + 1', and 'puppy' and 'young dog', have the same meaning and hence that the definitions are trivially true? But surely the whole point of a definition that encapsulates a successful analysis is that it is informative? When we considered the definition of water as H_2O, I suggested that someone could indeed understand the meanings of 'water' and 'H_2O' without knowing (at a certain time) that the definition was true: for them it could be informative. And are not the analyses discussed in Chapters 1 and 2 intended to be informative? Indeed, did you not find at least some of them informative? How could this be if the relevant meanings were not different—in the way that the meanings of 'water' and 'H_2O' are different? But if that is the case, then how can the definition be true?

Sense and reference

Many paradoxes arise because of an ambiguity in a key term. The paradox of analysis might seem to be no exception. Surely it cries out for a disambiguation of 'meaning'—for an analysis of 'meaning'! In a definition (recording an analysis) of the form '*A* is *B*', '*A*' and '*B*' must have the same meaning, in one sense of 'meaning', for the definition to be correct; but must have different meanings, in a different sense of 'meaning', for the definition to be informative. What are these two different senses of 'meaning'?

One answer is to distinguish between 'sense' and 'reference', which is a distinction that Frege introduced to account for the informativeness of identity statements, of which definitions are one kind. Frege's most famous example is the following:

(HP)   Hesperus (the Evening Star) is Phosphorus (the Morning Star).

'Hesperus' was the name given to the planet Venus as it appears in the evening, and 'Phosphorus' the name given to Venus as it appears in the morning. It came as a discovery to astronomers that Hesperus and Phosphorus were indeed one and the same heavenly body, namely, Venus. (HP) is thus both true and informative.

What Frege said is that 'Hesperus' and 'Phosphorus' have the same *reference* (they both refer to Venus) but different *senses*. A sense, according to Frege, expresses a 'mode of determination' or 'mode of presentation' of a reference. Venus can be presented to us in the morning, as reflected in our using 'Phosphorus' ('the Morning Star') to refer to it, or in the evening, as reflected in our using

3. **Phosphorus and Hesperus.**

'Hesperus' ('the Evening Star'). The identity statement can be informative insofar as we learn that the object referred to in one way is in fact the same object referred to in another way.

(HP) is not a definition, but Frege's distinction can clearly be applied in suggesting how successful analyses can be stated in true and informative definitions. Expressed in the form 'A is B', 'A' and 'B' must have the same reference for the definition to be correct but different senses for it to be informative. 'Water is H_2O', for example, could be seen as representing a correct chemical analysis in virtue of 'water' and 'H_2O' referring to the same substance, and as being informative to the extent that 'water' and 'H_2O' have different senses (along the lines suggested above).

I think that some such distinction between sense and reference is the first step in resolving the paradox of analysis, although the notion of 'sense' has generated enormous debate ever since Frege introduced the distinction and calls for clarification and elaboration. But something more is needed anyway, in my view, to resolve the paradox. Let us go back to Frege's analysis of 'Unicorns do not exist' as 'The concept "unicorn" is not instantiated'. It would be misleading to describe this as just two ways of conceiving the same thing, on the model of 'Hesperus is Phosphorus'. The point of the analysis is to correct *mis*understandings that we might have in thinking 'Unicorns do not exist'. The senses are not, as it were, on a par; and it might be better to think of the analysis as sharpening or refining the sense of 'Unicorns do not exist', bringing the senses into line by enriching our original understanding with the new conceptual resources upon which our analysis draws. If talk of 'sense' is intended to capture what we understand about something, then this can change over time, even when we use the same expressions, and analysis itself effects such change. In a nutshell, I think that analysis is informative by being *transformative*, and we need to give the idea of transformation a central role in our account of analysis. We have already illustrated the idea in Chapters 1 and 2, and we will be returning to it in what follows.

So do you know what I mean?

Moore's open question argument, we noted, makes a key
assumption: that if you understand the meanings of two phrases,
then you can immediately tell whether those meanings are the
same or not. In the light of the disambiguation of 'meaning' just
suggested, this assumption is only plausible, at best, for senses. If
this is right, then there is one way in which I can be said to know
what I mean: when I understand the senses of the expressions
I use, taken as implying the ability to tell whether those senses are
the same as those of any other expressions that I understand.
Correspondingly, there is one way in which you can be said to know
what I mean: when you understand the senses of the expressions
I use. And you can be said *not* to know what I mean when you do
not understand the senses of the expressions I use.

With the disambiguation of 'meaning' into 'sense' and 'reference'
in mind, however, there is another way in which you can be said
not to know what I mean, even when you understand the senses of
the expressions I use: when you do not know what the reference
is of at least one of those expressions. If I say 'My friend is coming',
for example, you may well ask 'Who do you mean?' if you do not
know to whom I am referring. To take a more extreme case, imagine
waking up in the middle of a pitch black room after having been
drugged and abducted, so that you have no idea where you are,
what time of the day or night it is, or even who you are. You may
well be able to utter a truth in saying 'I am here now', but do you
really know what you mean if you do not know what 'I', 'here' and
'now' refer to? If I am with you in the same state, then I do not
know what you mean, either.

For present purposes, though, the interesting cases concern what
we say when someone cannot provide relevant analyses and
definitions. In his later work, Moore came to stress that one can
understand the meaning of an expression without knowing its

analysis. Interpreting 'meaning' here as sense rather than reference, this might seem right: we can understand the sense of 'water', for example, without knowing that it is H_2O. In the light of what we have said about the transformative role of analysis, however, there is room for argument here. There would seem to be some grounds for claiming that someone does not 'really' know what they mean by 'water' if they do not know that it is H_2O. And correspondingly, if you do know what the relevant analyses and definitions are, and I do not, then there would be grounds for saying that you know better than me what I mean. The question 'Do you know what I mean?', then, itself has various meanings, and we need to know which meaning is meant before we can answer. It's all kind of like, 'well, it all depends'. Know what I mean?

Chapter 4
Are there limits to what we can say or think?

'You can't say that!' How many times have you been told that? Perhaps you were ranting about your boss to a close friend and suggesting what you might say at your next meeting. Or you are planning with your colleagues a presentation to a funding organization. You may also have been told, or have said to yourself, 'You can't think that!' Perhaps you are scared that you will mess up a presentation. Or you feel sure you will be beaten in a sports match by someone who has won against you on previous occasions. But you know that if you think those things, then your performance will suffer. Of course, the 'can't' in all these cases is not a logical 'can't'. There is an obvious sense in which you *can* say or think those things. The point is that you *can't* if you want something: to keep your job, to gain funding, to do a good presentation, or to win a match. The limits to what we can say or think in such cases, then, are determined by our aims and interests.

But are there *logical* limits to what we can say or think? It would be tempting to put it like this: are there things that we cannot say or think as a matter of logic? If we were to answer this question by stating what these things are, however, then we would be patently contradicting ourselves! So talk of 'limits' is better. If there are indeed limits to what we can say or think, then while we cannot show what these are by going beyond them (unlike showing, say, what the boundaries of an area are by overstepping it), we can indicate them from *inside* the domain of what can legitimately be said or thought. So what kind of limits might there be?

If what we can say or think is governed by our language, then the obvious strategy for answering this question is to determine the limits of our language. Ever since people began to reflect on their language, however, there has been scepticism about its adequacy in representing the world and expressing our beliefs, and some have certainly held that there are some beliefs—religious beliefs, for example—that cannot be properly expressed in language. This might suggest that while there are limits to what we can say, there are no corresponding limits to what we can think. (There may be other limits, but not ones entirely set by language.) But can we have thoughts that outstrip our ability to say what they are? And if not, then what are the limits of language that constrain both what we can say and what we can think?

Some difficulties in saying things

Let us return once again to Frege and Russell. In Chapter 1, we saw that Frege held that there was a fundamental distinction between object and concept. Objects are what fall under (first-level) concepts, and (first-level) concepts are what apply to objects (and to which in turn higher-level concepts apply). The most basic kind of thought we can have, according to Frege, involves applying a (first-level) concept to an object, such as in thinking that Gottlob is human, and such thoughts can be readily expressed in the logical system he created—his 'Begriffsschrift' ('concept-script'), as he called it. 'Gottlob is human', for example, can be formalized as 'Fa', with 'F' representing the concept of being human and 'a' the object that is Gottlob. Frege saw his Begriffsschrift as capable of expressing, in principle, every possible kind of thought. But how would we formalize his fundamental claim that there is a distinction between object and concept? We might express this in ordinary language by saying that no objects are concepts (or equivalently, that no concepts are objects), but it turns out that there is no way to represent this in Frege's Begriffsschrift. So if this claim is seen as expressing a true thought, then this is not a thought that can be expressed in Frege's logical language. It is a thought that seems to outstrip what we can say within such a language.

As we saw in Chapter 2, in proposing his theory of types Russell argued that a distinction should be drawn between objects, classes of objects, classes of classes of objects, and so on up the hierarchy. Once again, however, there is a problem in stating this distinction, as what can be said of objects cannot be said of classes of objects, or of higher-level classes, and vice versa. We can say that an object is a member of a certain (first-level) class—for example, that Gottlob is a member of the class of humans. We can also say that an object is *not* a member of a certain (first-level) class—for example, that Gottlob is not a member of the class of horses. But now imagine saying that a class is not an object (in order to try to express the distinction that Russell wants to draw)—for example, that the class of humans is not an object. This would be to say that the class of humans is not a member of the class of objects. But both these two classes are *first-level* classes, and a first-level class cannot be a member of another first-level class, according to Russell's conception of a hierarchy of classes. (A first-level class can be a *subclass* of another first-level class, but that is a different relation.) Such talk is therefore ruled out on Russell's view. Similar problems affect other attempts to express the distinctions reflected in Russell's hierarchy—for example, that an object is not a class, which would be to say that an object is not a member of the class of classes. But objects can only be members of classes of objects, not classes of classes of objects. So there are difficulties in stating the distinctions.

Let us take a simpler example to illustrate that the problem does not just affect what might seem more technical areas of philosophy. Consider our concept of being hungry. This concept applies to a certain *category* of objects, namely, those that are capable of eating, in other words, to animals. If Libby is a lapdog, then I can say, either truly or falsely, that Libby is hungry, and equally, either truly or falsely, that Libby is not hungry. But what if I ask 'Is this laptop hungry?' Answering 'yes' would suggest, absurdly, that it needs some food; but equally, answering 'no' might suggest that it has already eaten and does not need to be fed again for a while (Figure 4). Laptops, we want to say, are not the kind of thing that can be

4. Aren't you hungry?

either hungry or not hungry: the concept of being hungry is not one that applies to such things. But to say 'This laptop is not hungry' is not the right way to express this thought. If it makes no sense to talk of laptops being hungry, then it also makes no sense of talk of their not being hungry. The suggestion, then, is that what is wrong with saying that objects are not concepts, or that objects are not classes of objects, is similar to what is wrong with saying that laptops are not hungry.

What we have here is what we would now call a *category mistake*. Things fall into different categories and what can be legitimately said of things in one category cannot necessarily be said of things in a different category. To make *this* clear, though, needs special handling: we are in the territory, once again, where philosophical confusion is easily generated.

Introducing Ludwig Wittgenstein

Ludwig Wittgenstein (1889–1951) is arguably the greatest philosopher of the 20th century, though his ideas have provoked strong reactions. Born in Vienna, he studied aeronautical engineering at Manchester University before becoming interested in philosophy after reading Russell's *Principles of Mathematics* (which had appeared in 1903). That book had an appendix expounding Frege's ideas and Wittgenstein wrote to Frege asking to visit him, which he did in the summer of 1911. As Frege was by then getting old and had health problems, he recommended that Wittgenstein study with Russell in Cambridge. Wittgenstein worked with Russell until October 1913 when he went to live by himself in Norway before joining the Austrian army on the outbreak of war in July 1914. He served throughout the war but continued to work on his philosophical ideas. They were eventually published in his short book, *Tractatus Logico-Philosophicus*, in 1921 (translated into English in 1922), one of the most important yet frustratingly enigmatic texts in the history of philosophy.

In the *Tractatus*, Wittgenstein claimed to have solved in essentials all the problems of philosophy, and from 1920 to 1926 he taught in various schools in the Austrian countryside before returning to Vienna to help design a house for his sister Gretl. He was gradually tempted back into philosophy through contact with members of the so-called Vienna Circle, who had been greatly influenced by the *Tractatus*, and who were then applying and extending Wittgenstein's ideas, not always with Wittgenstein's approval. He finally returned to Cambridge in 1929, where he began to criticize his earlier ideas and assumptions, and to develop a new approach to philosophy. He was elected to a Fellowship at Trinity College and succeeded Moore as Professor of Philosophy in 1939, resigning in 1947. He published no further book in his lifetime but his writings were edited, translated and published after his death in 1951. These include *Philosophical Investigations* (mostly composed before 1945) and *On Certainty* (dating from the last two years of his life), the two most influential books of his later period.

Saying and showing

What drew Wittgenstein into philosophy was Russell's paradox, which Russell formulated in discovering the contradiction in Frege's system, as we saw in Chapter 2. Russell's answer was the theory of types, but Wittgenstein did not regard this answer as satisfying. On the other hand, he approved of Russell's theory of descriptions, although he drew his own conclusions from what he took as its message. As far as Frege's work is concerned, what Wittgenstein found here was a source of problems with which he grappled not just in his early work but throughout his life. As he makes clear in his preface to the *Tractatus*, Frege and Russell were the two most important influences on his thinking. So with our discussion in Chapters 1 and 2 in mind, we can now make sense of Wittgenstein's response to at least some of Frege's and Russell's ideas.

Let us begin with Russell's theory of types. Wittgenstein's basic objection is that Russell is indeed attempting to say something that cannot be said, at least meaningfully (if that theory is right). We have noted the difficulties in trying to state the distinction between objects and classes (and classes of classes, etc.). These difficulties arise because Russell wanted to outlaw talk of classes being members of themselves (which generates Russell's paradox): classes can only be members of higher-level classes. But to say that a class cannot be a member of itself is itself to violate the type-restrictions that Russell lays down. (If it is meaningless to say that a class is a member of itself, then it is equally meaningless to say that a class is not a member of itself.) Wittgenstein's response is to suggest that such things can only be *shown*, not said. (In German, the distinction is between *zeigen* and *sagen*.) That there is a distinction between object and class, or between object and concept, for example, cannot be *said*, but it can nevertheless be *shown* in an appropriate symbolism—by the fact that the relevant terms operate in different ways.

The basic idea here goes back to Frege (and may well have resulted from discussions that Wittgenstein had with Frege when he visited him for a second time in December 1912). As we have seen, Frege analyses the sentence 'Gottlob is human', for example, into the name 'Gottlob', representing an object, and the concept-word 'x is human', representing a concept. Frege calls names 'saturated' or 'complete' expressions, and concept-words 'unsaturated' or 'incomplete' expressions, because the latter have a gap—here marked by the variable 'x'—to indicate where the name has to go to yield a complete sentence. The difference between object and concept is thus reflected in the difference between 'saturated' names and 'unsaturated' concept-words. We use names to single out objects and concept-words to apply concepts to objects (in saying that something has a certain property). Names and concept-words, then, operate in different ways.

If 'Gottlob' and 'human', say, were the same kind of expression, then 'human is Gottlob' ought to be just as meaningful as 'Gottlob is human'. But only the latter has meaning. On Frege's account, this is because the logically significant expressions are 'Gottlob' and 'x is human' (not simply 'human'), which can only be put together ('Gottlob' slotting into the argument-place marked by 'x') to form the latter but not the former. The very nature of language, then, depends on this fundamental difference in the way that names and concept-expressions work, and this is something we implicitly understand in being able to use language at all. It is this that Frege is getting at when he stresses the distinction between object and concept, even though this cannot be adequately expressed by saying 'No objects are concepts'. Indeed, what I have just said in explaining Frege's ideas here is hardly captured in such an apparently simple sentence as 'No objects are concepts'.

Wittgenstein recognized what was at issue in Frege's discussion of the concept/object distinction and realized that the same problems arose in Russell's theory of types. The distinction between saying and showing allowed him to diagnose what was wrong: what Frege and Russell were attempting to *say* in drawing their distinctions of type can only be *shown* in our use of the relevant terms. Again, we can use our example of the concept of being hungry to illustrate the basic point. That this concept cannot apply to anything that is not an animal is *shown* in our use of the term 'hungry'. Any attempt to express this by saying such things as 'Laptops are not hungry' flouts the rules of meaning that govern our use of 'hungry' and fails to do justice to the category distinctions that are involved here.

The distinction between saying and showing is fundamental to the philosophy of the *Tractatus*—or so it seems. For now comes the twist in the tale, which has generated a great deal of controversy, especially in recent years. What about the distinction itself? Can we *say* what this distinction is, or can it, too, only be *shown*?

Let us explore this further by considering, first, Wittgenstein's conception of saying and, second, his conception of showing.

What is it to say something?

On Wittgenstein's view, a sentence, when used to express a sense, is a kind of *picture*: it presents a possible state of affairs—a way that the world could be. If that state of affairs does indeed obtain—if the world is indeed that way—then the sentence is true; if the state of affairs does not obtain, then the sentence is false. How does a sentence picture a possible state of affairs? It does so, according to Wittgenstein, by its elements being correlated with the objects of the state of affairs it represents and for those elements to be so related as to represent the relation between those objects. The sentence 'Iris is taller than Lulu', for example, pictures the possible state of affairs in which Iris is taller than Lulu, where 'Iris' refers to Iris, 'Lulu' to Lulu, and 'x is taller than y' represents the relation of being taller than. The sentence pictures this possible state of affairs in essentially the same kind of way in which the picture in Figure 5 does. Here the drawing of the first girl represents Iris, the drawing of the second girl represents Lulu, and the fact that the first is taller than the second represents Iris's being taller than Lulu.

Such an account presupposes that there are indeed objects to which the elements of the sentence refer. Those objects need not stand in the relations pictured by the sentence (in which case the sentence is false), but the objects have to exist for the sentence to have a sense. So what about sentences involving definite descriptions that lack a reference, such as 'The King of France is a philosopher'? It is here that Wittgenstein appeals to Russell's theory of descriptions. As we saw in Chapter 2, Russell interpreted such a sentence as 'really' about concepts—in this case, as saying that the concept "King of France" is uniquely instantiated and that whatever instantiates this concept also instantiates the concept

5. 'Iris is taller than Lulu.'

"philosopher". If this is right, then what has to exist for the sentence to have a sense (and to be either true or false) are the concepts involved here (including the logical concepts such as that of being instantiated).

In fact, however, these concepts may in turn be further analysable. The concept "King of France" might be analysable in terms of the concept of being a King and of the object that is the country

France, for example. What is necessary for a sentence to have a sense, then, is that all the elements of that sentence that represents *its ultimate analysis* have a reference. The ultimate analysis of a given sentence, however, may in fact be enormously complicated. Consider one of our other examples from Chapter 2: 'The average British woman has 1.9 children'. The full analysis of this sentence must make reference to every British woman and to each of their children (the claim then being that the total number of the latter divided by the total number of the former equals 1.9). If this sentence is to have the sense it does, then all of these people must exist.

Notoriously, however, Wittgenstein never gave an example of an ultimate analysis of a sentence, or even indicated the kind of analysis that one might expect. But he did insist that every sentence had an ultimate analysis and that the objects thereby revealed to exist (whatever they turned out to be) had to exist—as a logical condition for the sentence to have a sense. At some point the language we use must make contact with the reality it seeks to represent. This was a view that Russell shared, and to which he gave the name 'logical atomism': the possibility of analysis presupposes that there are 'atoms' of reality at the most fundamental level to secure a reference for all the elementary names that make up the sentence expressing the ultimate analysis.

Sense and senselessness

According to Wittgenstein, then, a sentence has a sense if and only if it pictures a possible state of affairs. Various conditions have to be met for sentences to picture possible states of affairs, but according to Wittgenstein, we cannot *say* what these are; rather, they are *shown* by the fact that the sentence does have the sense it has. So let us return to Frege's and Russell's attempts to express category distinctions. A sentence such as 'No concepts are objects', according to Wittgenstein, lacks a sense because it does not picture a possible state of affairs. If it means anything at all, then it is simply an attempt to *show* one of the conditions for sentences to have sense. Does this then mean that it is strictly speaking nonsense? Before answering this question, we need to explain a further distinction that Wittgenstein draws—between being senseless (*sinnlos*) and being nonsense (*unsinnig*).

To do this, let us consider another paradox—which, in philosophy, as we have already seen, is often a good way to motivate the need for certain distinctions. This is the paradox of inference (Box 4).

Box 4. The paradox of inference

Consider the following simple example of a logical inference:

> It is raining.
> If it is raining, then there are clouds in the sky.

Therefore: There are clouds in the sky.

This is a *valid* inference: if the two premises are true, then the conclusion is true. We can represent this inference schematically as follows, formalizing 'It is raining' by 'P' and 'There are clouds in the sky' by 'Q', and using '→' to represent the conditional 'If...then...':

> P
> P → Q

Therefore: Q

'Q' follows logically from 'P' and 'P → Q'. Logicians call the rule that licenses this inference '*modus ponens*', and it is one of the most basic rules of logical inference.

Let us now imagine someone objecting to this: 'Ah, so 'Q' only follows from 'P' and 'P → Q' *if we accept this rule*. So shouldn't you

(*continued*)

Box 4. Continued

make this rule explicit if you want to properly represent
the argument?' How might we state this rule? The obvious
suggestion would be to write '(P & (P → Q)) → Q' ('If P and (if P,
then Q), then Q'). The objector's point could then be put as
follows: our inference is only valid if this further proposition is
added as the missing premise in the argument. The argument
therefore needs 'completion' as follows:

$$P$$
$$P \rightarrow Q$$
$$(P \,\&\, (P \rightarrow Q)) \rightarrow Q$$
$$\overline{}$$

Therefore: Q

If we do this, however, then an infinite regress threatens. Should
we not add as a further premise '(P & (P → Q) & ((P & (P → Q)) → Q))
→ Q', and so on? How can we ever draw a valid inference? Can an
argument ever be completed?

What has gone wrong? The short answer is that '(P & (P → Q)) → Q'
should *not* be seen as a missing premise in the argument: the
inference in its original formulation is perfectly valid as it is.
The conclusion is indeed correctly inferred *in accord with* the
rule of *modus ponens*, but this rule should be seen as *governing*
the inference rather than as a separate element in it. For every
rule of inference there will be some corresponding *logical*
proposition, but such logical propositions have a quite different
status to the premises of an argument. (If an argument is
compared to a house built of bricks, then rules of inference are
like the mortar that holds the bricks together and not the
bricks themselves.)

In the *Tractatus*, Wittgenstein makes this point by saying that
logical propositions *lack* sense, in other words, are *senseless*. Unlike

'P', 'P → Q' and 'Q', all of which may have sense, '(P & (P → Q)) → Q' is senseless, precisely because it adds nothing to the inference. All it does is reflect that 'Q' can indeed be inferred from 'P' and 'P → Q', i.e., it reflects the rule of *modus ponens*. In our example, 'P' ('It is raining'), 'Q' ('There are clouds in the sky') and 'If P, then Q' ('If it is raining, then there are clouds in the sky') all have sense, and in exactly the way that Wittgenstein suggests: they all present possible states of affairs. '(P & (P → Q)) → Q', on the other hand, does not: it is true however the world may be. Logical propositions, according to Wittgenstein, are *tautologies*: they are true in every possible situation and as such *say* nothing about the world.

Wittgenstein distinguishes, however, between *senselessness* and *nonsense*. While logical propositions are senseless, they are not nonsense, since they nevertheless *show* something. '(P & (P → Q)) → Q' shows that one can infer 'Q' from 'P' and 'P → Q'. Take another example of a logical proposition, one of the form 'P or not P'. If you are told 'Either it is raining or it is not raining', then you learn nothing about the world, but this does show something—most notably, that these are exclusive options, as reflected in the fact that we call 'P or not P' the law of excluded middle.

Whatever one takes logical propositions to show, however, the key point is that they have a very different status from ordinary 'empirical' propositions, propositions that do tell us something about the world. Their tautologous character also distinguishes them from straightforward nonsense: they may not say anything, but they nevertheless show something—about our inferential practices.

Can nonsense show anything?

What, then, is nonsense? If what is senseless can nevertheless show something, then is nonsense to be understood as what cannot even show us anything? Or are there different types of nonsense? How should we see Frege's and Russell's attempts to express category distinctions? I have suggested that what Frege and Russell were trying to say can only be shown, according to Wittgenstein. But does this mean that sentences such as 'No concepts are objects' should be treated as a kind of logical proposition, and hence as senseless rather than nonsense?

The issues raised here have generated enormous controversy. When one considers the propositions of the *Tractatus*, one realizes that the vast majority fail to satisfy Wittgenstein's condition for having sense: they do not picture any possible state of affairs; and while some are logical propositions, most are not. This has led some commentators to distinguish two types of nonsense, literal nonsense and 'illuminating' nonsense. Illuminating nonsense does indeed show something, the 'ineffable' truths that Wittgenstein is supposedly trying to convey in describing the nature of language, logic and the world. Others, however, have urged that we take much more seriously Wittgenstein's own famous metaphor at the very end of the *Tractatus*—that his propositions should be seen as a ladder to be kicked away once one has climbed up to the correct viewpoint. Most of his propositions are indeed nonsense, strictly speaking, and the aim of the *Tractatus* is to help us think through to a full appreciation of this and its implications. Who is right?

Nonsense arises in many different ways, but what it typically involves or trades on is some kind of violation of the rules that govern the use of certain expressions. Violating grammatical rules might simply result in gobbledegook, such as 'peanutted aquamarines sloshed rebarbative', but the kind of nonsense that interests philosophers occurs when the sentence may be perfectly grammatical (at least on the surface) but where the conditions or limits of applicability of at least one key expression are transgressed, in other words, where semantical rules are violated. 'My laptop is hungry' would be a simple example: as suggested earlier, 'hungry' is not a predicate that applies to inanimate objects.

A sentence such as 'No concepts are objects' might seem like 'No whales are fish', and a sentence such as 'No class can be a member of itself' like 'No one can take a photo of themselves', but when we understand what confusions and paradoxes may arise, we realize that the similarities are misleading and that the first of the two sentences, in each case, is really just disguised nonsense. Clarifying this may require a lot of work, but the end result is not a reinterpretation of the sentence as making sense but a recognition of just why it should be regarded as nonsense. In recognizing this, however, we learn something about the conditions and limits of applicability of the relevant expressions, and to this extent something is shown. So there is truth on both sides of the controversy mentioned above. It is not the sentence itself that shows something, and in particular, it expresses no ineffable truth; but the process of elucidating why it is nonsensical does indeed show something—about certain fundamental features of the language we use. The same might be said about any attempt to state the distinction between saying and showing itself: what is meant here is shown by just the kind of elucidation that I have sought to provide in this chapter.

Is metaphysics nonsense?

Wittgenstein's *Tractatus* had a profound effect on the development of logical empiricism—or logical positivism, as it is also known—in the 1920s and 1930s. This is the movement that originated in the work of the Vienna Circle, whose members included Rudolf Carnap (1891–1970). What the logical empiricists took above all from Wittgenstein was his repudiation of metaphysics—at any rate, as suggested by a remark that Wittgenstein makes near the end of the *Tractatus*:

> The right method of philosophy would really be this: to say nothing except what can be said, that is, propositions of natural science—in other words, something that has nothing to do with philosophy—and then, whenever someone else wanted to say something metaphysical,

to show them that they had given no meaning to certain signs in their propositions.

Metaphysics is that branch of philosophy that is concerned with the fundamental nature of the world, or as it might also be characterized, with the most fundamental categories by means of which we think about the world, such as "object", "concept", "existence", "being", "substance", "space", "time", and so on.

The logical empiricists drew a fundamental distinction between 'analytic' and 'synthetic' propositions. Analytic propositions, they held, are propositions that are true or false solely in virtue of the meanings of the constituent terms. 'Green is a colour', for example, was regarded as true in virtue of the meaning of 'green'. Synthetic propositions, on the other hand, are true or false in virtue of the way the world is. 'This orchid is green' is a simple example: it is true if the orchid I am referring to does indeed have the property of being green. In offering an account of synthetic propositions, the logical empiricists appealed to what they termed the doctrine of verificationism: a proposition has meaning if and only if it can be *verified*, that is, its truth or falsity can in principle be determined by experience. To judge whether 'This orchid is green' is true or false, for example, we need to look at the orchid and see what colour it is.

The doctrine of verificationism built on Wittgenstein's conception of sense. A proposition has sense if and only if it pictures a possible state of affairs; if that state of affairs obtains, then the proposition is true, and if not, then it is false. What the logical empiricists added, as a further condition for a proposition to have sense (or meaning), is that we must be able to *verify* whether that state of affairs obtains or not. All empirical—or scientific—propositions were taken as falling into this category.

What about logical propositions? According to Wittgenstein, they are senseless, but nevertheless have a truth-value: they are true if they are tautologies, false if they are contradictions. Although they dropped talk of 'senselessness', the logical empiricists took Wittgenstein to have provided a convincing account of logical propositions. As they characterized it, logical propositions are 'analytic', since they are true or false in virtue of the meaning of the logical terms. The law of excluded middle, 'P or not-P', for example, is true in virtue of the meaning of disjunction and negation.

So what about metaphysical propositions? According to Frege, there are two basic kinds of thing in the world, objects and concepts, which are quite distinct from one another. So 'No concepts are objects' would be a good example of a metaphysical proposition. Yet, on Wittgenstein's account, this is strictly speaking nonsense. The same applies to all other metaphysical propositions: insofar as they neither picture possible states of affairs nor are logical, they are nonsense. The logical empiricists endorsed this view: metaphysical propositions are neither synthetic, since they cannot be verified, nor analytic, since they are not true or false solely in virtue of meaning, and are therefore meaningless.

In a famous paper entitled 'The Elimination of Metaphysics through Logical Analysis of Language', published in 1932, Carnap built on these views in arguing that logical analysis shows that metaphysical propositions are *pseudo-propositions*. While they may seem as if they have meaning, once we try to translate them into a logical language, we realize that they are meaningless. 'No concepts are objects' illustrates this, too. Carnap's own examples include some remarks that Martin Heidegger made in a lecture given in 1929 entitled 'What is Metaphysics?' Heidegger makes such statements as 'the Nothing is prior to the Not and the Negation' and 'The Nothing itself nothings' ('*Das Nichts selbst nichtet*'), which Carnap criticizes for wrongly treating 'Nothing' as a proper name instead of as a quantifier. As we have seen, to say 'Nothing is a unicorn', for example, would be to say that the concept "unicorn" has no instances, formalized in logic using the existential quantifier as '¬(∃x) Ux' ('It is not the case that there are any unicorns').

Carnap's attack on Heidegger has become a classic of uncharitable interpretation, and misses the point of what Heidegger was 'really' trying to say (not nothing!). But it illustrates how Carnap extended Wittgenstein's ideas by emphasizing the role to be played by a logical language, such as the one that Frege and Russell had developed. Formalizing propositions in a logical language offers a way of sieving out metaphysical propositions, which can then be emptied into the waste bin of nonsense. According to the logical positivists, metaphysics attempts to think beyond the limits of what can be meaningfully said or thought and needs to have its pretensions curbed and the nonsense it generates cleared up.

So are there limits to what we can say or think?

In the preface to the *Tractatus*, Wittgenstein wrote that his aim was to draw a limit to thought, or rather, as he put it, to the expression of thoughts, since the only way to draw this limit is from within language. For Wittgenstein, then, the limits to what we can think are indeed set by the limits of our language, and it was the task of the *Tractatus* to show this, if not in every detail then at least in broad outline. We have focused on one main kind of example to illustrate this—the case of category distinctions, such as Frege's object/concept and Russell's object/class distinction, which themselves provide constraints on our thinking. According to Wittgenstein, we cannot *say* what these distinctions are, but that they hold is *shown* in our (correct) use of the relevant expressions—proper names, concept-words, and class terms.

Any attempt to violate the grammatical or semantical rules of language results in nonsense, and the problems of philosophy, Wittgenstein felt, arise through misunderstanding of these rules—from the failure to understand the logic of our language, as he put it. Solving—or perhaps better, dissolving—these problems thus requires showing how these rules are violated. One way to do this—as Carnap advocated—is by showing how they do not arise in a 'Begriffsschrift' or logical language such as Frege and Russell envisaged. But Wittgenstein stressed that logical languages, too—and in this he differed from Carnap—can generate philosophical confusion of their own, as we have seen with Russell's paradox and the theory of types. So the construction of a logical language is not a panacea for all philosophical problems, but must itself be used with our philosophical purposes clearly in mind. There are indeed limits to what we can say or think, then, and while there may be difficulties in *saying* what they are, they can certainly be *shown* by carefully elucidating the complex workings of language.

Chapter 5
How can we think more clearly?

Analytic philosophy places great emphasis on clarity. But what does 'clarity' mean and how can we think more clearly? How does clarity connect with other virtues of analytic philosophy? In the Introduction to this book, I mentioned precision and rigour as two other virtues that have traditionally been seen as characteristic of analytic philosophy. But I also suggested that creativity, fruitfulness, and systematicity are also virtues, at least of the best analytic philosophy, and I have especially been concerned to show how analytic philosophy is conceptually creative. So how does clarity relate to all of this?

Taking stock

One way of getting clear about things is by taking stock. So let us see if we can start to answer these questions by reviewing some of the ideas that have been discussed so far in this book. Let us first return to one of the concepts explored in Chapter 1. Do we think clearly about infinity? The concept of infinity is certainly invoked in ordinary thinking. Yet, when we consider infinite sets, we realize that it is by no means as simple as might be supposed. Whether or not you were convinced by the arguments offered in introducing transfinite numbers, I hope that at least the general point was conveyed—that there may be various criteria for the use of a given concept, which can come apart in non-standard cases, thereby engendering new or modified concepts. One way to think more clearly, then, is to appreciate the criteria involved in our use of concepts and hence to recognize that there may be more specific concepts that need distinguishing.

We can immediately see how clarity and creativity connect in this particular kind of case: greater clarity in our thinking can be achieved through the conceptual creativity involved in introducing finer-grained concepts. That these new concepts are finer-grained also illustrates the virtue of precision of expression: armed with more subtle distinctions, we can say what we mean more accurately. In talking of two sets having the same number, we can say that we mean it in the sense that their members can be correlated one–one, for example. And we can see here, too, the connection between the virtues of clarity and precision: clarity of thinking is manifested in precision of expression.

Understanding the criteria for the use of concepts goes hand in hand with appreciating the range and limitations of their applicability, concerning which greater clarity of thinking can also be achieved. We saw this illustrated in discussing Russell's paradox in Chapter 2 and Wittgenstein's response to Russell's own solution, the theory of types, in Chapter 4. Typically, concepts apply legitimately only within a certain domain and under certain conditions: the concept of being hungry, for example, only applies (in its literal sense) to a certain category of objects, namely, animals. Any application outside this domain yields nonsense. In this case, we might feel that there is some tension between clarity and creativity, since applying concepts *outside* their usual domain might be viewed as almost a paradigm of creativity. The short answer here would be to admit that sense can sometimes be established *through* nonsense, but that understanding of how this sense is established is nevertheless required if we are to think clearly about this.

It is in the role played by interpretive analysis, however, that we can see the strongest connection between clarity, precision, and creativity. In Chapter 3, I stressed the way in which interpretive analysis is *transformative*: by rephrasing a sentence using richer conceptual resources, or by understanding how it can be so rephrased, we can think more clearly about what is meant. As Frege's analysis of existential and number statements and Russell's theory of descriptions suggest, what might look as if it is about objects may turn out to be 'really' about concepts. Here clarity, precision, and creativity all come together.

I have not said much yet about the other virtues mentioned above: rigour, fruitfulness, and systematicity. Fruitfulness is closely connected with creativity, and rigour (of argumentation) and systematicity are features more of theories than of individual analyses. We will return to these shortly.

Introducing Susan Stebbing

L. Susan Stebbing (1885–1943) published what was in effect the first textbook of analytic philosophy in 1930 and did more than anyone else to promote the development of analytic philosophy in Britain. Born in London, she was educated at Girton College, Cambridge, and King's College London, and taught in both Cambridge and London for the rest of her life. In 1933 she became the first woman Professor of Philosophy in Britain, and she also served as President of the two main philosophical societies in Britain, the Aristotelian Society (in 1933–34) and the Mind Association (in 1934–35). She co-founded in 1933 the journal *Analysis*, which has remained one of the flagships of analytic philosophy to this day, and she played a key role in inviting leading members of the Vienna Circle to Britain and encouraging discussion of their ideas. As we will see in Chapter 6, analytic philosophy developed into the tradition that we know today by bringing together—albeit in creative and critical tension—the ideas of Russell, Moore, and Wittgenstein in Britain and the logical empiricism of the Vienna Circle, with roots of both in the earlier work of Frege.

By her own account, Stebbing was 'converted' to analytic philosophy when Moore commented on a paper she read to the Aristotelian Society in 1917, and she kept in touch with Moore for the rest of her life. Her textbook, *A Modern Introduction to Logic*, appeared in 1930. With over 500 pages, it covered many of the topics that are now associated with analytic philosophy, such as the nature of logic and logical inference, the analysis of propositions, the theory of descriptions, scientific methodology (concerning e.g. causation and induction), definition, and abstraction. The book quickly established itself as a guide to the new developments, and a second edition came out in 1933. Her later books addressed themselves to a more general audience. She published two much shorter books on logic, *Logic in Practice* (1934) and *A Modern Elementary Logic* (1943), and two books which can justly be regarded as among the first books of critical thinking, *Philosophy and the Physicists* (1937) and *Thinking to Some Purpose* (1939), both published by Penguin. Stebbing died in September 1943.

A sensible view of metaphysics?

Stebbing was one of the first philosophers to respond to the wholesale attack on metaphysics by the logical empiricists. Her main criticism was that any philosophical view—including logical empiricism itself—makes certain presuppositions, and these will include metaphysical presuppositions. Frege assumed a basic distinction between objects and concepts, for example, and Wittgenstein found himself admitting that the world is composed of simple objects that *must* exist to ensure that we can use language meaningfully. Logical empiricism, too, makes certain presuppositions, which are far from uncontroversial. Take the claim that there is an absolute distinction between analytic and synthetic truths, for example. Is this an analytic or a synthetic truth? It seems to be neither true in virtue of the meaning of 'analytic' and 'synthetic' (unless 'synthetic' is defined, unhelpfully, as 'non-analytic') nor an empirical truth. That there is a distinction between matters of 'meaning' and matters of 'fact' seems like just the kind of metaphysically-loaded assumption that the logical empiricists should be criticizing.

Stebbing was honest in the assessment of her own—Moorean—philosophical approach. In attempting to spell out its presuppositions, she came to the conclusion that they, too, could not be justified. Like Wittgenstein, she recognized that this approach presupposed, most notably, that any analysis must ultimately come to rest in a set of basic facts. But as the debate raged in the 1920s and 1930s about what these basic facts were, there was increasing scepticism about whether any such ultimate level could be reached. In response, a distinction came to be drawn—by Stebbing, among others—between logical or 'same-level' analysis and metaphysical or 'new-level' analysis.

Take one of Stebbing's examples: 'Every economist is fallible' (which is more true now than ever before!). This would be formalized in logic as '$(\forall x)(Ex \rightarrow Fx)$' ('For all x, if x is an economist, then x is fallible')—it has the same logical form as 'All horses are animals', which we discussed at the end of Chapter 2. This gives us the *logical analysis*, but we might still ask what the basic facts are that make such a proposition true. One possibility would be to see it as reducible to a conjunction of specific facts such as that Karl Marx is fallible, John Maynard Keynes is fallible, Muhammad Yunus is fallible, and so on. This would be to give us a *metaphysical analysis*. Logical analysis is 'same-level' analysis since it only gives us a (supposedly) equivalent formulation. Metaphysical analysis is 'new-level' analysis because it (supposedly) shows us what is 'out there' to which our propositions are ultimately to be taken as referring.

With this distinction drawn, it now becomes possible to reject metaphysical analysis while retaining logical analysis. Doubts about metaphysical analysis, then, need not affect the legitimacy of logical analysis. To return to one of our earlier examples, suppose that someone is puzzled about how we can say that unicorns do not exist. It might be enough to point out that what we 'really' mean is that the concept "unicorn" is not instantiated; we need not attempt to give any 'deeper' metaphysical analysis. However, we could also allow a more modest role for metaphysical analysis by recognizing that what analysis we give is relative to our purposes. Talk of what a committee does, for example, could be reduced to talk of what the individual members of that committee do, without having to explain any further what it is to be a person. We need only take the analysis far enough, in other words, to solve a particular problem; we can reject the idea of there being any 'ultimate' analysis. This is the approach that Stebbing took in her later work, and seems to offer a sensible view of metaphysics.

Thinking to some purpose

Consider an example that Stebbing gives in discussing what she calls 'reflective thinking'—as opposed to 'idle reverie'—in the first chapter of *A Modern Introduction to Logic*. A non-swimmer is daydreaming on some rocks at the seaside when a shout makes them realize that the tide is coming in and that their way back along the beach is now cut off. Knowing that they cannot swim, they look to see how they might scramble further up the rocks. From the green lines on the rocks they work out where the high water mark is likely to be and notice a ledge above it that should make them safe, so they form the decision to climb up to this ledge. Such reflective thinking, Stebbing writes, is 'directed': it is essentially concerned with solving a problem, in this case, how to avoid drowning. It also counts as *logical* to the extent that it moves, legitimately, from premises such as 'The tide is coming in', 'I cannot swim', 'I am below the high water mark', and 'That ledge is above the high water mark' to the conclusion 'I must climb up to that ledge'.

In her later work Stebbing talks more of 'purposive' than of 'directed' thinking, but the idea is the same and it becomes a guiding theme in all her subsequent writings. Indeed, 'Purposive

Thinking' forms the title of the first chapter of *Logic in Practice*, a very short (100-page) non-technical introduction to logic and critical thinking which appeared in 1934. She begins here by characterizing purposive thinking as 'thinking directed to answering a question held steadily in view', and goes on to elucidate what is typically involved in such thinking. The idea is also reflected in the title of what is perhaps her best-known book, *Thinking to Some Purpose*, published on the eve of the outbreak of the Second World War. To think effectively, she writes, is to think to some purpose, governed by the question we are trying to answer and the circumstances in which we are doing so. Our thinking, she stresses, always involves our whole personality and is determined by the context in which we find ourselves.

Although the details of particular acts of purposive thinking will vary enormously, there are a number of generic features that they typically have in common. We can illustrate these by taking Stebbing's example of the person on the rocks. First, there must be apprehension of the relevant empirical facts. In this case, the person must recognize that the tide is coming in and perceive the rocks around them, for example. Second, they must have knowledge of relevant laws or generalizations about the world, such as that the tide reaches a high point each day and that this can be roughly worked out by the green lines on the rocks. Third, they must know facts about themselves, such as their inability to swim but their ability to climb, for example. Fourth, they must understand what the problem is, that they will drown if they stay where they are, and what possible solutions there are, such as clambering sideways along the rocks in the hope of finding a way out or just climbing up higher to wait until the tide goes back down again. Fifth, they must be able to reason, that is, to draw conclusions from premises, such as in the way indicated above. Finally, they must be able to use and understand language. In this case, they must understand what someone meant in shouting to them, as well as have the ability to express their beliefs and desires in language in thinking to themselves. (Here is where the case differs from many other cases, where explicit use of language may play a far greater role.) Of all these generic features, Stebbing's main concern is with the last two, so let us look in a little more detail at each in turn.

Logical thinking

Logical thinking involves inferring one proposition, called the conclusion, from one or more other propositions, called the premise or premises. Such inference or argument is *valid* if it is not possible for the premises to be true and the conclusion false, in other words, if the conclusion follows from the premises. A simple example of a logical inference, having the form 'P, P → Q, therefore Q', was given in Chapter 4. Here is another example:

> The tide is coming in.
> If the tide is coming in, then the sea will reach the high water mark.

Therefore: The sea will reach the high water mark.

We can see such inferences as involved in the reflective thinking of the person on the rocks. Indeed, we could reconstruct their thinking as a whole chain of such inferences. Having drawn the conclusion that the sea will reach the high water mark, for example, they might continue their reasoning as follows:

> I am below the high water mark.
> If I am below the high water mark, then the sea will reach me.

Therefore: The sea will reach me.
> If the sea will reach me, then I must climb above the high water mark.

Therefore: I must climb above the high water mark.

This chain of reasoning makes essential use of the rule of *modus ponens*, as discussed in Chapter 4. This is one of the most fundamental rules of logic, but it is by no means the only rule, and there might be many other ways of reconstructing the reflective thinking of the person on the rocks. But however we reconstruct it, we must ensure that the inferences are valid. This is not to say that the premises must all be true. All that is necessary is that *if* the premises are all true, *then* the conclusion is true.

How capable are we of logical thinking? Let us stay with this example of inferring in accord with the rule of *modus ponens*, which permits us to infer 'Q' from 'P' and 'If P, then Q' ('P → Q'). Central to this is our understanding of conditionals of the form 'If P, then Q', where P is called the antecedent and Q the consequent. So how well do we understand conditionals? Consider the Wason selection task, as described in Box 5. How would you answer?

Box 5. Wason selection task

Imagine there are four cards lying on the table, each of which has a letter on one side and a number on the other. What you see is this:

Which (one or more) of the cards do you need to turn over to test whether the following conditional is true?

If there is a vowel on one side, then there is an odd number on the other.

If you answered that you must turn over the cards with the A and the 3 on them, then you would be in good company: tests have confirmed that most people do indeed give this answer, at least when first asked. But it is nevertheless wrong. You do not need to turn over the card with the 3 on it, as regardless of what is on the other side, it cannot *falsify* the conditional. If it has a consonant on the other side, then it is simply irrelevant to testing the conditional; and if it has a vowel, then it does not provide a counterexample.

There is a sense in which, if the card with the 3 on it has a vowel on the other side, then it *confirms* the conditional—in being a positive instance of it. This may partly explain why people have often thought that this card must be turned over. But to test the conditional, all we *need* to consider are those possible cases in which it might be falsified. If the card with the A on it has an even number on the other side, then this would falsify the conditional, so this card must indeed be turned over. The vast majority of people get this right straight off. But so must the card with the 6 on it be turned over, as if this has a vowel on the other side, then it also falsifies the conditional. We do not need to turn over the card with the M on it, as this is also irrelevant to testing the conditional. So the right answer is to turn over the cards with the A and the 6 on them. It might take more explanation from me to convince you of this, or more thinking on your part to recognize this, but what is also interesting about this selection task is that most people can indeed be brought to see that this is the right answer, even if they gave the wrong answer at first. This is a very significant result. *Even if we make logical errors in practice or on certain occasions, we can be taught to recognize them—and this demonstrates that we are capable of logical thinking.*

This particular test was devised and first used by the psychologist Peter Wason in 1966—well after Stebbing's time. But it is an implicit assumption of Stebbing's work that we are capable of logical thinking. Logicians throughout the ages have been concerned to formulate the rules of reasoning and to identify common fallacies, and Stebbing discusses many of them in her writings. Some of the rules may be less deeply entrenched in our reasoning than *modus ponens*, and some of the fallacies less readily explained than the mistake commonly made in the Wason selection task. But the key point here is that all these rules and fallacies can in principle be explained to (almost) all of us. Clear thinking requires respecting the rules of logic and avoiding fallacies, so that one way to think more clearly, as Stebbing herself urged and helped promote, is to study logic and learn about the various mistakes of reasoning that can be made.

Critical thinking

Stebbing discusses logical thinking in detail in her textbooks on logic. It is also a theme in *Thinking to Some Purpose*, but here the concern is much broader. On the inside cover of the 1948 reprint that I have it is described as 'a manual of first-aid in Clear Thinking'. Today we would call it a book of critical thinking. If I was asked to explain how analytic philosophy caught on in the wider intellectual community (in other words, outside the realm of university teachers of philosophy), then I would point to the influence of books such as Stebbing's *Thinking to Some Purpose*. It makes as strong a case as one could wish for the kind of clear thinking that is one of the cardinal virtues of analytic philosophy.

The book contains various chapters in which particular kinds of unclear thinking are diagnosed and remedies suggested. In chapter 6, for example, Stebbing discusses what she calls 'potted thinking'—thinking that relies on slogans or snappy, compressed statements. If fresh thinking has preceded it, then it may be harmless, but if all it does is save us the trouble of proper thinking, then it is dangerous. In today's world of text messaging and tweeting, there is a greater need than ever before for the kind of interpretive analysis characteristic of analytic philosophy, in making sense of potted thinking—whether it unpacks the fresh thoughts that were indeed condensed or, instead, shows up its confusions, simplifications, or pretensions.

Stebbing also discusses the roles played by metaphor, analogy, parable, allegory, and simile in our thinking, and the ways in which these may mislead us. Metaphors are far more pervasive in language than one might initially realize. Stebbing used a metaphor in coining the term 'potted thinking', for example, and in the same vein, we also speak metaphorically when we call an idea 'half-baked'. (And I have used two other metaphors in this last sentence alone.) Many metaphors are now dead (to use another metaphor!), in the sense that the comparison that originally motivated it has been forgotten and the term has acquired a life of its own (to mix metaphors!). Dead metaphors, as well as freshly minted metaphors, to the extent that they are recognized as such, may be relatively harmless. The dangers lie in the grey area in between, where the comparison embodied in the metaphor may influence our thinking without our being sufficiently aware of it. 'Analysis' is itself such a metaphor, as we will see in Chapter 6.

Analogies can be used either to illustrate something, such as an argument or claim, or as a form of argument itself. In the latter case, we talk of argument by analogy. Something may have a certain set of properties, F, G, and H, say, as well as a further property P. We may then discover that something else has the properties F, G, and H, and infer—on the assumption that the analogy holds—that it also has property P. As a heuristic device, this may be useful in directing us to further properties that something may have, but as an argument it clearly only works if the analogy holds. Like metaphors, then, analogies can be misleading if taken too far. They can help train our thinking but soon run out of steam!

The same can be said of parables, allegories, and similes, which are widely used in all kinds of writing—for example, in Chinese literature, where there is a rich tradition of making points subtly and indirectly, and in religious texts. One of the most famous examples in philosophy is Plato's allegory of the cave in the

6. Plato's allegory of the cave.

Republic, offered as a picture of the human condition. Plato
imagines a group of people chained up at the end of a cave so that
they can only see the wall in front of them. Behind them is a fire
which casts shadows on the wall when things appear and move
above another, lower wall between them and the fire (for the basic
idea, see Figure 6). The prisoners take the shadows for reality.
A second example is the trio of similes that Francis Bacon uses
in Aphorism 95 of his *New Organon*:

> The men of experiment are like the ant, they only collect and use;
> the reasoners resemble spiders, who make cobwebs out of their
> own substance. But the bee takes a middle course: it gathers its
> material from the flowers of the garden and of the field, but
> transforms and digests it by a power of its own. Not unlike this is
> the true business of philosophy; for it neither relies solely or chiefly
> on the powers of the mind, nor does it take the matter which it

gathers from natural history and mechanical experiments and lay
it up in the memory whole, as it finds it, but lays it up in the
understanding altered and digested.

Likening the 'true' philosopher to the bee is a wonderful image,
but we are presumably not meant to infer that philosophers also
have nasty stings (though we might then take comfort in the
thought that they can only sting once before they die).

The longest chapter in *Thinking to Some Purpose* is called
'Slipping away from the point'. As well as discussing various
logical fallacies, Stebbing addresses the issue of ambiguity.
That the same word may have more than one meaning is not a
problem in itself: context will often resolve any ambiguity or
polysemy. If someone were to ask you in a city centre where the
nearest bank was, you are unlikely to interpret this as referring
to a river bank rather than a financial institution. The danger
lies in slipping from one meaning to another during the course
of an argument.

So how can we think more clearly?

Stebbing's book discusses a whole range of ways in which we can
be misled—from logical fallacies and potted thinking to analogies
and ambiguity. In drawing our attention to them, she shows
how we can think more clearly by avoiding them. So a short
answer to the question 'How can we think more clearly?' would
be: read—and learn the lessons from—a book on critical thinking
such as *Thinking to Some Purpose*. We can also learn to think
more clearly by making explicit all the premises of our arguments,
so that it is easier to ensure—and for others to recognize—that our
conclusions are validly inferred. So here the corresponding advice
would be: read—and learn the lessons from—a book on logic. We
can also see here how the virtues of clarity of thinking and rigour
of argumentation connect.

7. One cannot draw from the same bank twice.

Setting out our argumentation more carefully also helps us to investigate what else follows from our assumptions and how the various things we believe hang together. It may enable us to uncover implicit assumptions and to detect inconsistencies, facilitating a better understanding of our beliefs and improving their coherence. Rigour of argumentation, then, also connects with the virtues of fruitfulness and systematicity.

We can also think more clearly by drawing finer-grained distinctions—*where appropriate*. Stebbing stresses that drawing sharper distinctions is not necessarily to think more clearly, if the topic does not permit sharp distinctions. It all depends on the context and the purpose of the thinking. Seeking a definition of 'analytic philosophy' that enables us to sharply distinguish analytic from non-analytic philosophy provides a good example, as we will see in the next—and final—chapter.

Chapter 6
So what is analytic philosophy?

I said in the Introduction to this book that my aim was to take you on a thought-thinking trip rather than a sight-seeing tour. In the subsequent chapters we have explored five themes that illustrate analytic philosophizing as it was pursued by Frege, Russell, Moore, Wittgenstein, and Stebbing. We have asked certain questions and considered how the philosophers concerned answered them. As I hope has emerged, there are various similarities and differences between their respective views and approaches. But is there anything in common that could be taken to characterize analytic philosophy as a whole? I have argued that analytic philosophers prize clarity and precision. Would it not be a great irony if they couldn't characterize their own discipline?

In my view, it is a mistake to try to define analytic philosophy in terms of any set of doctrines that are shared by all and only analytic philosophers. (Moore's open question argument might well be applicable here.) Certainly, what counts as analytic philosophy today is so broad-ranging and open-ended that any attempt to do so would be futile. An alternative suggestion is to characterize analytic philosophy, more loosely, as held together by family resemblances, to use an idea from Wittgenstein's later philosophy. This, too, is problematic, since between any two philosophers, further philosophers can always be found to construct a chain of family resemblances, so that every philosopher might end up counting as an analytic philosopher.

A more sophisticated answer would be to enrich the idea of a family resemblance by embedding it in a detailed historical story that explains the arguments, doctrines, and theories as they actually developed in the debates that were inspired by those recognized as the founders of analytic philosophy. Someone counts as an analytic philosopher to the extent that they actively and self-consciously contribute to these ongoing debates. I am very sympathetic to this approach, and have attempted to reflect it, in part, in this book—in discussing the way that Russell sought to solve the paradox he discovered in Frege's work, for example, and the distinction between saying and showing that Wittgenstein came to draw in criticizing both Frege and Russell.

Telling such a historical story, however, is not incompatible with identifying certain features of analytic philosophy that can be helpful in understanding its main character and distinguishing it from other kinds of philosophy. What I have also tried to show in this book is that analytic philosophy is above all a *way* of doing philosophy, exemplifying certain virtues and using the new methods that came from the development of modern logic.

Analysing 'analysis'

As I suggested in the Introduction, the obvious way to characterize analytic philosophy is in terms of its use of analysis. Given that 'analysis', in some form, has always played a role in philosophy, however, this just pushes the problem onto the question of what forms of analysis are employed in analytic philosophy. In Chapter 3, I distinguished 'interpretive' from 'decompositional' and 'regressive' analysis, and suggested that, while all three are present in analytic philosophy, it is the former that is especially characteristic of Frege's and Russell's work, and with which Moore was especially concerned in raising questions about analysis.

8. Penelope unravelling her web.

In Chapter 5, I mentioned Stebbing's view of how metaphors can mislead us. Talk of 'analysis', in fact, provides an excellent example of this. One of the original meanings of the ancient Greek term '*analusis*', from which 'analysis' derives, was 'unravelling': the prefix '*ana*' meant 'up' and '*lusis*' meant 'loosening' or 'separating'. We find this meaning in Homer's *Odyssey*, for example, where Penelope is reported as 'unravelling' by night the web of thread for a shroud she was weaving by day, in order to stave off her suitors, having promised to make a decision on whom to marry (in Odysseus' long absence) when the web was complete (Figure 8). The term was then extended, metaphorically, in talking of 'unravelling' or 'dissolving' problems. (Penelope, after all, found a brilliant solution to her own problem!) In ancient Greek geometry, this soon acquired a more technical sense, referring to the process of working back to more basic theorems and principles, or simpler geometrical constructions, by means of which the relevant problem (proving a given theorem or constructing a certain figure) could then be solved. This is analysis in the 'regressive' sense, although exactly how it was meant to work has been disputed down the ages.

When Greek terms were translated into Latin, '*analusis*' was rendered as '*decompositio*', and both terms were transliterated into English as 'analysis' and 'decomposition'. The two English terms were sometimes used as synonyms, sometimes with slightly different meanings—with 'decomposition' having more of the meaning of 'breaking down'. (Something similar happened, most notably, with 'fantasy' and 'imagination', 'ethics' and 'morality', 'psychological' and 'mental', the first in each pair of terms deriving from the Greek, the second from the Latin. Sometimes they are used or understood more or less synonymously, sometimes as having rather different meanings. There is a similarly fascinating, philosophically significant, and long story in each case.) To the extent that 'analysis' and 'decomposition' were treated as synonyms, however, the connotations of 'decomposition' were projected back onto 'analysis', or perhaps more accurately put, reinforced the decompositional connotations that 'analysis' already had and obscured its other meanings. In other words, 'analysis' gradually took on more of the sense of 'decomposition', so that, today, the decompositional sense is indeed the one that is most associated with 'analysis'.

However, the other senses lived on, and in particular, the key idea of analysis as 'solution' or 'dissolution' rather than 'decomposition' has also (to use yet another metaphor) infused conceptions of analysis ever since. Take the case of 'analytic' geometry, for example, which was created by Descartes and Fermat in the 17th century. What happens here is that geometrical problems are solved using the resources of algebra and arithmetic. A line, for example, is represented by the equation $y = ax + b$, where 'x' and 'y' give you the coordinates in plotting the line on a graph, with 'a' representing the gradient of the line and 'b' the point where the line cuts the y-axis (where $x = 0$). Problems that cannot be solved within Euclidean (ancient Greek) geometry, which came to be called 'synthetic' geometry by way of contrast, can be readily solved within analytic geometry.

In analytic geometry, the geometrical problems are solved by 'translating' them into the language of arithmetic and algebra. And here we can also see how 'interpretive' analysis plays a role. Lines, circles, curves, and so on, must first be 'interpreted' as equations, and the geometrical problems correspondingly reformulated, before arithmetic and algebra can be applied in solving them. The idea here can be generalized: problems need to be interpreted in some form before the resources of a relevant theory or conceptual framework can be brought to bear. And this is exactly what is involved in analytic philosophy: the propositions to be analysed—those that give rise to the philosophical problems to be solved or dissolved—need to be rephrased in a richer conceptual framework or formalized in an appropriate logical theory. Analytic philosophy, then, is 'analytic' much more in the sense that analytic geometry is analytic than in any crude decompositional sense.

Let me stress again, though, that all three of the forms of analysis I have distinguished are typically involved in any actual example or project of analysis. Indeed, insofar as 'decomposition', 'regression' and 'interpretation' are themselves metaphors, they really just reflect different aspects or dimensions of the process of solving problems. We solve problems in all sorts of ways and combinations of ways. We may have to break them down into smaller parts that are easier to handle, to identify things we already know that may help us, and/or to reformulate them to open up new approaches. It is not surprising, then, that analysis is far more complicated than any particular metaphor is able to capture.

But if 'analysis', in its widest sense, just means problem-solving, then doesn't all philosophy count as analytic? And if what we now call analytic philosophy is just 'analytic' in some extra special sense, then what is that sense that makes it appropriate to emphasize analysis in its self-description? The short answer here is the use it made of modern logic—the quantificational logic developed by Frege, Russell, and others—together with all the new techniques that emerged in its wake and the greater understanding of the relationship between logic and language that this generated. Just as analytic geometry transformed geometry by utilizing the powerful tools of arithmetic and algebra, so analytic philosophy transformed philosophy by utilizing the powerful tools of quantificational logic and theories of meaning.

Introducing later analytic philosophy

We have focused in this book on some of the main ideas of five of the founders of analytic philosophy. Thinking through these ideas gives a better sense of analytic philosophizing, in my view, than a whistle-stop tour of the whole terrain. But a lot has happened since the early years of analytic philosophy. So how has it evolved subsequently? Staying with the theme of analysis, let me outline two central strands in its later development by distinguishing two different ways in which the earlier conceptions and practices of analysis were transformed and extended.

In Chapter 5, we saw how a distinction came to be drawn—by Stebbing, among others—between logical or 'same-level' analysis and metaphysical or 'new-level' analysis. This distinction opened up the possibility of accepting the first while rejecting the latter—and especially, rejecting the assumption that there must be some final, definitive metaphysical analysis. This is the approach that was taken by what are now often called, though rather misleadingly, 'ordinary language philosophers' or 'linguistic philosophers', working especially in Oxford in the 1950s and 1960s, but including Wittgenstein, who rejected some of the key ideas of his *Tractatus* in developing his later philosophy in Cambridge in the 1930s and 1940s.

The main fruits of Wittgenstein's later thinking are contained in his *Philosophical Investigations*, the main part of which was completed by 1945 but only published in 1953, after his death. Wittgenstein continues to be concerned with what distinguishes sense from nonsense, but he rejects his earlier assumption that there is a single logic—essentially that formulated by Frege and Russell—that underlies our use of language, as well as his earlier view that propositions have sense if and only if they picture possible states of affairs. Instead he emphasizes the multiplicity of what he calls our 'language-games', each of which is governed by its own 'logic' or 'grammar'—the term he now prefers—understood as the set of rules according to which the language-game is played.

Philosophy, on Wittgenstein's new conception, consists in gaining an 'overview' of the grammar of our language-games, aimed at clearing away the misunderstandings that may arise. In §90 of the *Investigations*, Wittgenstein writes:

> Our examination is ... a grammatical one. And this examination sheds light on our problem by clearing away misunderstandings. Misunderstandings concerning the use of words, arising, among other things, from certain analogies between the forms of expression in different areas of our language.—Some of them may be removed by replacing one form of expression by another; this can be called an "analysis" ["Analysieren"] of our forms of expression, for the process sometimes resembles decomposition.

As this suggests, Wittgenstein's method might also be characterized as a form of 'analysis', although I think that he is being slightly misled himself in thinking of analysis too much in 'decompositional' terms. But it certainly counts as what Stebbing called 'same-level' analysis and I have called 'interpretive' analysis.

The second, rather different conception of analysis that developed after the Second World War was influenced more by Frege's and Russell's work than by Moore's and Wittgenstein's, and in particular, by the type of analysis exemplified in their logicist project. Recall Frege's definitions of the natural numbers in terms of classes discussed in Chapter 1. These are not definitions that any 'ordinary' speaker is likely to come up with; as we have seen, they were intended to provide a deeper understanding of arithmetic by using the richer conceptual resources of the new logic. Carnap came to call this 'explication', which he characterized as involving the *replacement* of an ordinary, vague term by a more precise, scientifically defined term—in the way that we might replace the everyday concept of warmth by the more exact concept of temperature defined in physics, or our ordinary concept of water by the more precise concept of H_2O defined in chemistry.

When the Nazis came to power in Germany in 1933, Carnap—together with other logical empiricists—emigrated to the United States, and the more 'scientific' conception of philosophy that they advocated took root there. Philosophy came to be seen as continuous with natural science, so that analysis, correspondingly, was viewed in a more scientific spirit, eventually opening the way—despite its repudiation in the heyday of logical empiricism—for reinvigorated metaphysical analysis.

After the Second World War, then, analytic philosophy can be seen as dividing into two main strands, one developing the approach of Moore and Stebbing, and the other building on the work of Frege and Russell, with Wittgenstein's *Tractatus* having differing influences on both. Let us look at each strand in a little more detail.

Ordinary language philosophy

Besides Wittgenstein, three philosophers stand out as representatives of 'ordinary language philosophy': Gilbert Ryle (1900–76), J. L. Austin (1911–60), and P. F. Strawson (1919–2006), all of whom were based in Oxford. Ryle's work epitomizes the move from new-level to same-level analysis in the development of analytic philosophy. In his 'Systematically Misleading Expressions' of 1932, he assumed that every proposition has a 'correct' logical form; but by the time he published his most influential book, *The Concept of Mind*, in 1949, he focused on charting what he called the 'logical geography' of our concepts. It was Ryle who popularized the idea of a 'category mistake', the central argument of his book being that the view, introduced by René Descartes in the 17th century, that the mind inhabits the body as a 'Ghost in the Machine', as Ryle described it, was a category mistake: what it makes sense to say about mental phenomena does not necessarily make sense to say about physical events, and vice versa. His book offered an account of a wide range of our concepts of mental phenomena, exploring their logical connections.

If Ryle was the Oxford Wittgensteinian, then Austin was the Oxford Moorean. His paper, 'A Plea for Excuses', published in 1956, offers the best introduction to his philosophical approach. He here addresses that perennial philosophical conundrum: do we have free will or is everything we do determined? Taking Moore's line in seeking to distinguish the different questions that might be asked here, Austin suggests that the supposed opposition breaks down into a number of far more specific distinctions, which play out in much subtler ways in the concrete contexts in which the terms are applicable. Consider the range of adverbs we use in describing how someone has acted in a not entirely 'free' way, such as 'inadvertently', 'mistakenly', 'accidentally', 'absent-mindedly', 'unintentionally', 'carelessly', 'automatically', 'aimlessly', and 'purposelessly'. Is there really a single overarching distinction between acting freely and being determined? I shall (deliberately) leave you free to make up your own mind about this!

Austin laid the foundations for what we now know as speech act theory. He emphasized the different kinds of things that we *do* with words. In saying 'I promise', for example, I am not just saying something (picturing a possible state of affairs), but *performing* the act of promising: Austin called this a 'performative' utterance. Strawson took up this idea of a speech act in criticizing Russell's theory of descriptions (as first presented in 'On Denoting' of 1905) in an influential article he published in 1950 entitled 'On Referring'. According to Strawson, if there is no King of France, then the statement that the King of France is a philosopher should be regarded as neither true nor false, not false as Russell had claimed. I am not *asserting* that there is one and only one King of France, but *presupposing* it as a condition for asserting something *about* this person. Assertion and presupposition are speech acts, something that we do in *using* language, and Strawson's basic charge against Russell is that he focused on sentences and not on our uses of sentences.

Strawson's later work is characterized by a return to metaphysics, but one that he calls 'descriptive' rather than 'revisionary', aimed at clarifying the fundamental conceptual framework by means of which we think about the world. In *Analysis and Metaphysics*, published in 1992, he distinguishes between 'connective' and 'reductive' analysis and endorses the former: the philosophical elucidation of a concept consists in explaining its often complex connections to other concepts.

Ideal language philosophy and scientific philosophy

Let me single out three philosophers to give a sense of developments in analytic philosophy in post-war America: W. V. O. Quine

(1908–2000), Donald Davidson (1917–2003), and Hilary Putnam (1926–2016). Quine's most influential paper is 'Two Dogmas of Empiricism', published in 1951, in which he attacked the logical empiricists' distinction between analytic and synthetic propositions as well as their reductive conception of analysis, according to which synthetic propositions are ultimately verified by sensory experience. According to Quine, there is no clear distinction between matters of 'meaning' and matters of 'fact', and he proposed an alternative view on which our whole 'web of beliefs', as he called it, is empirically tested as a whole.

Quine agreed with Carnap, however, that the role of philosophy was to 'explicate' our ordinary concepts and beliefs by 'translating' or—as he put it—'regimenting' them into a suitable logical language. But while Carnap had seen this as a way of eliminating metaphysics, Quine regarded this—as Russell had done earlier—as revealing our 'real' ontological commitments, in other words, as showing what our best scientific account tells us about what things there are in the world. In Strawson's terms, Quine endorses 'revisionary' metaphysics, albeit informed by the results of the natural sciences.

Davidson was highly influential in another major development in post-war analytic philosophy: the construction of theories of meaning. Frege's work is generally taken as the starting-point, but Frege's concern was primarily with mathematics—with how mathematical language expresses the thoughts and arguments it does. Davidson was concerned with constructing a theory of meaning for natural languages, in all their richness and complexity. This is now a huge research industry, as both philosophers and linguists seek to understand how the various elements of language work, from pronouns to metaphors. One contribution Davidson made was to the analysis of sentences about actions and events, which he suggested showed how we are committed to an ontology of events—in other words, that events should be taken as existing in the world just as Frege, for example, thought that objects and concepts exist.

Davidson also identified and rejected what he called the third dogma of empiricism: the view that one can distinguish between conceptual scheme and empirical content. According to Davidson, we can make no sense of someone's having a completely different conceptual scheme from our own. If true, then this has implications for the question we considered in Chapter 3: we can only know what another person means if we have some common conceptual understanding, rooted in our shared engagements with the world. Grasp of meaning, the ability to interpret others, and participation in collective activities are fundamentally interconnected.

Putnam has had a significant influence on American philosophy across a wide range of fields. I shall just mention here his thought experiment about Twin Earth, since this has relevance for the issue we considered in Chapter 3 concerning the 'analysis' of water as H_2O. Twin Earth is imagined as exactly like our Earth except that what looks and tastes like water is actually not H_2O but a different chemical compound, say, XYZ. According to Putnam, and the 'intuitions' about what to say here that he hopes to invoke, someone on Earth would be referring to and thinking about H_2O, and someone on Twin Earth would be referring to and thinking about XYZ, even if neither of them knew what the chemical compound was of the watery substance they were experiencing. So meanings and thoughts are partly individuated by what lies outside us, in the external world, a thesis that is called 'externalism'. If this is right, then there is a response to the paradox of analysis: the 'external' meaning helps secure the correctness of 'Water is H_2O', and yet you can still learn something when you discover this. Putnam captured his basic idea with the slogan 'meanings just ain't in the head'. The debate about externalism has raged ever since, both inside and outside people's heads.

How did analytic philosophy get its name?

We now see the origins of analytic philosophy as lying in the work of Frege, Russell, Moore, and Wittgenstein in the four decades around the turn of the 20th century. (Frege's *Begriffsschrift* was published in 1879, Wittgenstein's *Tractatus* in 1921.) Yet we do not find the term 'analytic philosophy' being used to refer to even part of what we now recognize as the analytic tradition until the early 1930s. The term does not appear, for example, in what I suggested is the first textbook of analytic philosophy—Stebbing's *A Modern Introduction to Logic*, published in 1930. We should not find this surprising, however, since it takes a certain amount of time for any movement or tradition to establish itself sufficiently to be conceptualized as such and for any name to catch on.

What may be surprising, though, is that the term is first used in *criticizing* analytic philosophy. The Oxford philosopher R. G. Collingwood (1889–1943) uses it in his *Essay on Philosophical Method* of 1933, in attacking the view according to which philosophy seeks only to analyse what we already know, a view which is attributed to Moore and Stebbing. For Collingwood, 'analytic philosophy' was intended as a derogatory term, suggesting a narrow-minded conception of philosophy. As we saw in discussing the paradox of analysis in Chapter 3, the question of how analyses can be informative is indeed a fundamental issue, so there is something to Collingwood's criticism. However, as I hope I showed, appreciating the *transformative* character of analyses offers an effective response to the paradox (a response, in fact, that we can find in Collingwood's own *Essay*).

The group of philosophers to which Moore and Stebbing belonged did indeed have a name in the 1930s—the Cambridge School of Analysis. The name reflected the inspiration that Russell's programme of analysis and Wittgenstein's views on analysis had on their work. So it was entirely appropriate to use the term 'analytic philosophy' as an alternative name, understood more positively. In the second half of the 1930s the term was extended to include the logical empiricists, who had also been influenced by Russell and Wittgenstein; but it was only after the Second World War that the term really caught on. By then it was also used to include both ordinary language philosophy and the new forms of ideal language philosophy and scientific philosophy developing in the States.

During the 1950s both the influence that Frege had on Russell, Wittgenstein, and Carnap, and the importance of his ideas for the project of constructing theories of meaning began to be appreciated, and analytic philosophy was 'backdated' to include him. Since then the canon has been expanding more and more, both backwards, sidewards, and forwards, and related philosophical traditions such as American pragmatism have been co-opted as well. (No one has yet been fired from the canon!) What began as a set of ideas and methods rooted in logic, philosophy of mathematics, and ethics, has now expanded through philosophy of language, philosophy of science, and philosophy of mind to all areas of philosophy. For every branch of philosophy, there is now an 'analytic' version, not just analytic metaphysics and analytic aesthetics (dating from the 1950s) but analytic Marxism, analytic phenomenology, and analytic feminism, for example, and I have even seen the term 'analytic dogmatic theology' being used! The name 'analytic' has caught on to such a degree that one might wonder what does not now count as analytic philosophy, at least in Western philosophy. To what is it opposed?

Analytic and continental philosophy

In 1958, a conference was held at Royaumont in France to which various analytic philosophers were invited to encourage dialogue with French philosophers. The conference was not a great success. Gilbert Ryle read a paper in which he talked of the wide gulf that had opened up between Anglo-Saxon and Continental philosophy. By 'Anglo-Saxon' philosophy he meant analytic philosophy and by 'Continental' philosophy he meant phenomenology, in particular. Since then the meaning of 'Continental philosophy' has broadened to include other traditions such as hermeneutics, existentialism, deconstruction, and indeed all kinds of Western philosophy from Kant onwards that are not analytic. The division has become one of the most entrenched and pernicious in contemporary philosophy. It illustrates, though, how traditions (like political parties) are partly formed and maintain themselves in mutual opposition.

As Bernard Williams once famously remarked, distinguishing between 'analytic' and 'continental' philosophy is like dividing cars into front-wheel-drive and Japanese; one term is methodological or operational, the other geographical. The supposed contrast involves a kind of category confusion, and is neither exclusive nor exhaustive. Recognized analytic philosophers such as Frege, Wittgenstein, and Carnap, for example, were brought up—and in Frege's case, spent his whole life—in German-speaking countries. And 'continental' philosophy employs forms of analysis as well. There are also many philosophical traditions, such as pragmatism, not to mention all the various non-Western traditions, that are hard to classify as either. However, just as we can unpack the metaphor of 'analytic', so too we can unpack the metonym of 'continental'. 'Continental philosophy' is an umbrella term for a range of traditions that have their origins—unlike analytic philosophy—*primarily* in the work of philosophers based in continental Europe. The founder of phenomenology was Edmund Husserl (1859–1938), for example, and key figures in the development of hermeneutics include Friedrich Schleiermacher (1768–1834) and Hans-Georg Gadamer (1900–2002). Existentialism has been most associated with the work of Jean-Paul Sartre (1905–80) and Simone de Beauvoir (1908–86), but has roots further back in the work of Søren Kierkegaard (1813–55), Friedrich Nietzsche (1844–1900), and Martin

9. A philosopher driving a front-wheel-drive Japanese car.

Heidegger (1889–1976). Jacques Derrida (1930–2004) has been the guiding spirit of deconstruction.

All the traditions that make up 'continental philosophy' have little in common beyond, negatively, their (supposed) opposition to analytic philosophy, and, positively, their all being, in some sense, responses to Kant's philosophy (though this would also include analytic philosophy). Since this book is about analytic philosophy, I will say no more about continental philosophy directly but instead consider some of the criticisms that continental philosophers, among others, have made of analytic philosophy, which have helped maintain the supposed opposition.

What is wrong with analytic philosophy?

The criticisms that continental philosophers have made of analytic philosophy, as well as those that analytic philosophers have made of continental philosophy, have frequently involved caricatures of the views they oppose. In Box 6 I have listed some of the main differences that have been claimed to hold between analytic and continental philosophy, all of which are caricatures, although—like all caricatures—they contain some element of truth that makes them plausible. Some concern method and style, with which we have been concerned throughout this book and to which I will return in the final section. I shall say something about the

---

Box 6. Some caricatures of the analytic/continental divide

Analytic philosophy	Continental philosophy
Uses analytic methods	Uses synthetic methods
Clear, precise, rigorous	Suggestive, allusive, playful
Logical argumentation	Sceptical of powers of reason
Problem-based	Text-based
Concern with truth	Concern with meaning
Scientific/scientistic	Anti-scientific/anti-scientistic
Naturalist	Non-naturalist
Realist	Idealist
Universalist	Relativist
Rationalistic	Humanistic
Ahistorical/anti-historical	Historical
Apolitical	Political

---

other differences here, under the two broad headings of the relationship of analytic philosophy, first, to natural science, and second, to history.

Especially over the last three or four decades analytic philosophy has been seen and criticized as both scientistic and naturalist. Scientism is the view that the natural sciences provide the model for explanation and understanding in other fields, including philosophy. Naturalism comes in two main varieties. In its stronger form it is similar to scientism, holding that everything can ultimately be explained by natural science. In its weaker form, it holds that there is nothing over and above the natural world—in other words, it rejects all appeals to anything 'supernatural'.

From Russell and the logical empiricists onwards, there has been a strong tradition within analytic philosophy that can certainly be described as 'scientific', in its respect for the methods and results of the natural sciences and in its weak naturalism. But that is not the same as being scientistic and strongly naturalist, though some analytic philosophers are that as well. It depends on one's view of the place of logic and metaphysics in all this. Many philosophers of mind today draw on and engage with the latest work in biology, cognitive science, neurology, and psychology, and many philosophers of language are in continual dialogue with linguists, among others. But they do so in a critical spirit and will use other methods than those of the natural sciences, so 'scientistic' is too strong a term to use even for them.

There is also a different strand that goes back to Frege, Moore, and the early Wittgenstein, who all rejected scientism and naturalism, although the later Wittgenstein is a naturalist in the weaker form. Frege conceived numbers as logical objects, understood as *non*-natural objects, for example, and Moore was a non-naturalist about ethics. The debate between naturalism and non-naturalism is a major one in all areas of contemporary analytic philosophy, so it would be wrong to see either position as characteristic of analytic philosophy.

In my view, there is one fundamental objection to scientism (and strong naturalism), which can be stated like this. Any science makes presuppositions, and it has traditionally been one of the primary tasks of philosophy to subject these to critical examination, tasks that require different methods to those of science itself. Analytic philosophy is well placed to do this, but not uniquely so. Phenomenologists, in particular, have offered a powerful critique of scientism, in arguing that the whole project of natural science, and the theoretical attitude it requires, needs to be understood as emerging from what Husserl called our 'life-world' ('*Lebenswelt*'), comprised of our everyday human practices and pre-theoretical attitudes and beliefs. In my view, analytic philosophy has not fully learnt the lessons of phenomenology, so this is one area where criticisms of analytic philosophy are justified.

The other main, though related area in which I would say that criticisms of analytic philosophy are justified concerns its attitude to history. Analytic philosophy has often been accused of being 'ahistoricist' and even 'anti-historicist'. Like naturalism, historicism comes in various forms, the strongest of which claims that philosophy is essentially historical and needs to be understood and pursued as such, and the weakest of which simply claims that knowledge of history is useful in pursuing philosophy. Few dispute the latter, but the former is far more controversial. Many analytic philosophers, and certainly the early ones, did indeed reject historicism in its strongest forms. Philosophical problems, it was assumed, are timeless, and while it might be useful to see how previous philosophers sought to solve them, fresh attempts can always be made, such as by drawing on the latest logical or scientific theories.

Let us grant that there are some philosophical problems that are universal, if not exactly 'timeless'—because they are rooted in such

fundamental human activities as counting and inferring.
We can also agree that solutions to these problems may involve
the fashioning of new conceptual tools. Nevertheless, historical
understanding will still be required. For the new concepts and
solutions will need to be explained and this will involve making
clear how they are related to other concepts and solutions, both
past and present. As philosophical debates proceed, engagement
with previous views is inevitable.

Philosophical views, too, make presuppositions, as we saw in
Chapter 5. These may not be clear at the time the views are first
formulated or debated; but sooner or later they will need to be
made explicit, if the debates are to progress. It may require a
certain historical distance to identify these presuppositions, so
here again is an area where historical understanding is needed.

Historical understanding may also be required in unpacking the
metaphors, analogies, parables, allegories, and similes that also
play a role in philosophy, as I hope I have illustrated in clarifying
the idea of analysis itself; and to these we might add all the
allusions and references—for example, to the ideas of past
thinkers—that we also find in philosophical writing. Derrida
(one of the continental philosophers mentioned above) has drawn
our attention to what he calls the 'margins' of philosophy—to
footnotes, prefaces, letters, interviews, casual remarks, and so
on—where a lot of 'unofficial' thinking takes place, which may
shed light on what is 'officially' said. Here again is where the work
of the historian comes into play.

Analytic philosophers often criticize historians of philosophy for
'merely' being concerned with what a past philosopher meant or
thought, focusing on interpreting texts, while their concern, they
say, is with what is true, focusing on solving philosophical problems.
But these two concerns are not as distinct as they suppose. If we
are to interpret what someone means as charitably as possible,
then we will need to know what is true, and any evaluation of their

views will certainly require this. And solving problems and finding out what is true may be fostered by working through the solutions and views that others have offered, which will require understanding what they meant. Analytic philosophy and history of philosophy need each other.

Lack of historical self-consciousness is arguably the biggest blind-spot in analytic philosophy. Not being overawed by tradition may be essential in making conceptual innovations, but establishing and defending those innovations requires locating them in the historical space of previous views. Continental philosophy offers rich resources for understanding this historical space—and for uncovering presuppositions, unpacking metaphors, deconstructing assumptions, contextualizing attitudes, and so on. Here is where analytic philosophy would benefit most, in my opinion, from deeper engagement with continental traditions.

So what is good about analytic philosophy?

On the account that I have offered in this book, analytic philosophy has its origins in the development and use of modern logic by Frege, Russell, and others. Philosophical problems are solved by translating the problematic sentences into logical language, making clearer what they 'really' mean. I described this process as involving interpretive analysis, as well as the regressive and decompositional forms of analysis that have always been present in philosophy. Interpretive analysis has been fundamental to analytic philosophy ever since, opening up questions about the nature of meaning and the relationship between logic and language that have been central themes throughout its history. So the first thing I would say is good about analytic philosophy is the deeper understanding it has fostered of the complex and myriad ways in which language works.

The development of modern logic has changed the philosophical landscape irrevocably. Before Frege, logicians had only been able to analyse a small subset of the inferences we make in everyday and scientific thinking. Building on Frege's work, logical and semantic theory has been further developed to deepen our understanding of the whole range of our conceptual and reasoning practices. It has also enabled philosophers to set out arguments as rigorously as possible, identifying all the premises and rules of inference that allow the conclusion to be validly drawn. By reconstructing arguments offered in the past, philosophers can demonstrate their validity or else show where they fail or what missing premises are needed. Applying logic—and the ideas of analytic philosophy, more generally—has deepened our understanding of the history of philosophy, mathematics, and science, both Western and non-Western.

Let us return, though, to the virtues which I mentioned at the beginning of this book, and which have been themes in the subsequent chapters. I hope that I have shown how clarity of thinking, precision of expression, and rigour of argumentation came to be regarded as central virtues in analytic philosophy, and justified my own belief that they are indeed virtues. I have also sought to illustrate how analytic philosophy is conceptually creative, something that deserves more recognition. When one looks back at the history of analytic philosophy, one realizes just how intellectually fruitful its conceptual innovations have been. Systematic work has also been done, from Frege's and Russell's logicist project to contemporary theories of meaning. But analytic philosophy also lends itself to more piecemeal contributions, such as in analysing specific concepts or reconstructing or criticizing particular arguments. A wide range of conceptual and logical tools have now been developed to assist the analytic philosopher's work, and what is first used in one domain has been applied in other fields.

In recent years, analytic philosophers, at least in some quarters, have become more historically self-conscious and increasingly willing to engage in dialogue with other philosophical traditions, from ancient Chinese philosophy to French deconstruction, and these developments are to be welcomed. As I have indicated, analytic philosophy has also ramified into all areas of philosophy, from logic and philosophy of mathematics to theology and critical thinking, and there is exciting work being done, drawing on, refining, and enlarging its methodological toolbox. The future of analytic philosophy is clear, even if its precise nature and contours are a matter of argument.

References and further reading

For the most comprehensive, multi-authored account of the nature, origins, and development of analytic philosophy, see:

Michael Beaney (ed.), *The Oxford Handbook of the History of Analytic Philosophy* (Oxford: Oxford University Press, 2013).

Chapter 3 contains a detailed chronology of analytic philosophy and Chapter 4 an extensive bibliography.

There is a book series on the history of analytic philosophy published by Palgrave Macmillan (<http://www.palgrave.com/gp/series/14867>), now comprising over thirty volumes. There are books on both central figures such as Bertrand Russell and Ludwig Wittgenstein as well as relatively neglected philosophers such as Bernard Bolzano, G. F. Stout, Susan Stebbing, and F. P. Ramsey. Other volumes focus on constituent traditions of analytic philosophy, such as Polish analytic philosophy, and the relationship between analytic philosophy and other philosophical traditions such as phenomenology.

The online *Stanford Encyclopedia of Philosophy* (https://plato.stanford.edu) is a wonderful resource, often the first place to go to on any philosophical topic or philosopher.

I make selections from all of these in recommending further reading in what follows.

The translations of the two passages from Wittgenstein's work that appear in Chapters 4 and 6 are my own.

Chapter 1: How many things are there?

The main text introduced in this chapter is:

Gottlob Frege, *Die Grundlagen der Arithmetik* (Breslau: W. Koebner, 1884); tr. as *The Foundations of Arithmetic* by J. L. Austin (Oxford: Blackwell, 2nd edn. 1953).

The other book mentioned, in which Frege first presented his logical theory, and which marks the single most important origin of analytic philosophy, is:

Gottlob Frege, *Begriffsschrift* (Halle: L. Nebert, 1879); tr. by T. W. Bynum in *Conceptual Notation and Related Articles* (Oxford: Clarendon Press, 1972).

Selections from both of these works (including the key passages discussed in both this chapter and Chapter 2), together with selections from Frege's other writings, are contained in:

Gottlob Frege, *The Frege Reader*, ed. M. Beaney (Oxford: Blackwell, 1997).

A good introductory book on Frege is:

Joan Weiner, *Frege Explained* (Chicago: Open Court, 2004).

A fuller account is provided in:

Michael Beaney, *Frege: Making Sense* (London: Duckworth, 1996).

Two chapters of the *Oxford Handbook of the History of Analytic Philosophy* are also relevant here. Gottfried Gabriel ('Frege and the German background to analytic philosophy') shows how Frege's key conception of number statements as assertions about concepts was anticipated by Johann Herbart (1776–1841), and Tyler Burge ('Gottlob Frege: some forms of influence') discusses Frege's influence on subsequent philosophy.

Galileo's paradox appears in:

Galileo Galilei, *Dialogues Concerning Two New Sciences* (1638), tr. by H. Crew and A. de Salvio (New York: Dover, 1954), pp. 31–3.

Cantor's diagonal argument was first published in 1891:

Georg Cantor, 'Über eine elementare Frage der Mannigfaltigkeitslehre', *Jahresbericht der Deutschen Mathematiker-Vereinigung*, 1, pp. 75–8; tr. in W. Ewald (ed.), *From Kant to Hilbert: A Source Book in the Foundations of Mathematics* (Oxford: Oxford University Press, 1996), vol. II, pp. 920–2.

For further discussion of the conceptual creativity involved in Cantor's development of transfinite arithmetic, on which I have drawn in this chapter, see:

Michael Beaney and Robert Clark, 'Seeing-as and mathematical creativity', in B. Harrington, D. Shaw, and M. Beaney (eds), *Seeing-as and Novelty* (London: Routledge, forthcoming).

Chapter 2: How can we speak of what does not exist?

The three texts mentioned in introducing Bertrand Russell are the following:

Bertrand Russell, *The Principles of Mathematics* (Cambridge: Cambridge University Press, 1903; 2nd edn. 1937, repr. London: Routledge, 1992);

Bertrand Russell, 'On Denoting' (1905), *Mind*, 14: 479–93; repr. in *Logic and Knowledge*, ed. R. C. Marsh (London: George Allen & Unwin, 1956), pp. 39–56;

A. N. Whitehead and Bertrand Russell, *Principia Mathematica*, 3 vols. (Cambridge: Cambridge University Press, 1910–13; 2nd edn. 1925–7); abridged as *Principia Mathematica to *56* (Cambridge: Cambridge University Press, 1962).

References and further reading

However, for the most accessible account of Russell's philosophy of mathematics, see:

Bertrand Russell, *Introduction to Mathematical Philosophy* (London: George Allen & Unwin, 1919).

Chapter 16 explains his theory of descriptions, more clearly than in his original paper of 1905 ('On Denoting').

For an overview, in his own words, of Russell's philosophy as a whole, see:

Bertrand Russell, *My Philosophical Development* (London: George Allen and Unwin, 1959; repr. Unwin Paperbacks, 1985).

The two other works referred to in this chapter are by Frege, one of them *The Foundations of Arithmetic*, introduced in Chapter 1 (see the references for that chapter), and the other:

Gottlob Frege, *Grundgesetze der Arithmetik* (Jena: H. Pohle, vol. 1 1893, vol. 2 1903); tr. as *Basic Laws of Arithmetic* by P. Ebert and M. Rossberg (Oxford: Oxford University Press, 2013).

As in the case of Whitehead and Russell's *Principia Mathematica*, most of this is highly technical, but there plenty of passages where Frege explains his logical and philosophical ideas: some of the key passages are translated in *The Frege Reader* (see the references for Chapter 1).

There is a Very Short Introduction to Russell (originally published in 1996):

A. C. Grayling, *Russell: A Very Short Introduction* (Oxford: Oxford University Press, 2002).

The following collection contains discussions of various aspects of Russell's philosophy, including his logicist project and his theory of descriptions, with a helpful introduction by the editor:

Nicholas Griffin (ed.), *The Cambridge Companion to Bertrand Russell* (Cambridge: Cambridge University Press, 2003).

For a more advanced treatment of the theory of descriptions, see:

Graham Stevens, *The Theory of Descriptions: Russell and the Philosophy of Language* (Basingstoke: Palgrave Macmillan, 2011).

In the account offered in Chapter 2, I have drawn on the following:

Michael Beaney, 'The Analytic Revolution', in A. O'Hear (ed.), *The History of Philosophy* (Cambridge: Cambridge University Press, 2016), pp. 227–49.

A talk based on this paper was given at the Royal Institute of Philosophy in London in January 2015 in a series on the history of philosophy (<https://www.youtube.com/playlist?list=PLqK-cZS_wviD2G4wi3YbaIuRlkJPjB01L>).

Chapter 3: Do you know what I mean?

The citation from Alexander Pope is taken from Part II of *An Essay on Criticism* (1711), lines 297–300.

I say much more about the three conceptions of analysis distinguished in this chapter in my entry on 'Analysis' in the *Stanford Encyclopedia of Philosophy* (see the references for Chapter 6).

Three texts by G. E. Moore are mentioned in this chapter. The first is:

G. E. Moore, *Principia Ethica* (Cambridge: Cambridge University Press, 1903; 2nd edn. 1993, ed. T. Baldwin).

The other two texts, 'A Defence of Common Sense' and 'Proof of an External World', can be found in the following edition:

G. E. Moore, *Selected Writings*, ed. T. Baldwin (London: Routledge, 1993).

On Moore's philosophy, the best place to start would be:

Thomas Baldwin, 'George Edward Moore' (2004), *The Stanford Encyclopedia of Philosophy*, <https://plato.stanford.edu/entries/moore/>.

On Moore and Russell's rebellion against British idealism, more specifically, there is a helpful chapter in the *Oxford Handbook of the History of Analytic Philosophy* by Nicholas Griffin ('Russell and Moore's revolt against British idealism').

The classic source for Frege's distinction between sense (*Sinn*) and reference (*Bedeutung*) is:

Gottlob Frege, 'Über Sinn und Bedeutung' (1892), *Zeitschrift für Philosophie und philosophische Kritik*, 100: 25–50; tr. by M. Black in *The Frege Reader*, ed. M. Beaney (Oxford: Blackwell, 1997), pp. 151–71.

A useful book on Frege's distinction and its place in his philosophy is:

Mark Textor, *Frege on Sense and Reference* (London: Routledge, 2011).

I also discuss the distinction, and its relationship to the paradox of analysis, in *Frege: Making Sense* (see the references for Chapter 1) and in the following:

Michael Beaney, '*Sinn*, *Bedeutung* and the Paradox of Analysis', in M. Beaney and E. Reck (eds), *Gottlob Frege: Critical Assessments of Leading Philosophers*, 4 vols. (London: Routledge, 2005), vol. IV, pp. 288–310.

Chapter 4: Are there limits to what we can say or think?

The key text discussed in this chapter is:

Ludwig Wittgenstein, *Tractatus Logico-Philosophicus* (1921), tr. C. K. Ogden and F. P. Ramsey (London: Routledge, 1922); also tr. D. F. Pears and B. McGuinness (London: Routledge, 1961; 2nd edn. 1974).

The other texts referred to in this chapter are Russell's *Principles of Mathematics* (see the references for Chapter 2) and the following:

Ludwig Wittgenstein, *Philosophical Investigations*, tr. G. E. M. Anscombe (Oxford: Blackwell, 1953; 4th edn. 2009, tr. rev. by P. M. S. Hacker and J. Schulte);

Ludwig Wittgenstein, *On Certainty*, ed. G. E. M. Anscombe and G. H. von Wright, tr. D. Paul and G. E. M. Anscombe (Oxford: Blackwell, 1969);

Rudolf Carnap, 'Überwindung der Metaphysik durch logische Analyse der Sprache' (1932), *Erkenntnis*, 2: 219–41; tr. as 'The Elimination of Metaphysics through Logical Analysis of Language' by A. Pap in A. J. Ayer (ed.), *Logical Positivism* (Glencoe, IL: The Free Press, 1959), pp. 60–81;

Martin Heidegger, 'What is Metaphysics?' (1929), tr. by D. F. Krell in *Basic Writings: Revised and Expanded Writings* (London: Routledge, 1993), pp. 93–110; also tr. by W. McNeill in *Pathmarks* (Cambridge: Cambridge University Press, 1998), pp. 82–96.

So much has been written on Wittgenstein over the last seventy-five years that it is hard to know where to start in suggesting further reading. For an account of the *Tractatus* that focuses on the themes introduced in the present chapter, I recommend the chapter by Michael Kremer in the *Oxford Handbook of the History of Analytic*

Philosophy ('The Whole Meaning of a Book of Nonsense: Reading Wittgenstein's *Tractatus*').

If I had to choose a single book to introduce someone to Wittgenstein's philosophy, from his earliest work to his last writings, I would suggest this:

William Child, *Wittgenstein* (London: Routledge, 2011).

And if I had to choose a single collection, I would recommend the following for its comprehensive coverage:

Hans-Johann Glock and John Hyman (eds), *A Companion to Wittgenstein* (Oxford: Wiley Blackwell, 2017).

On logical empiricism, a good place to start would be:

Richard Creath, 'Logical Empiricism' (2017), *The Stanford Encyclopedia of Philosophy*, <https://plato.stanford.edu/entries/logical-empiricism/>.

Chapter 5: How can we think more clearly?

The books referred to in this chapter by Susan Stebbing are:

L. Susan Stebbing, *A Modern Introduction to Logic* (London: Methuen, 1930; 2nd edn. 1933);

L. Susan Stebbing, *Logic in Practice* (London: Methuen, 1934);

L. Susan Stebbing, *Philosophy and the Physicists* (London: Methuen, 1937);

L. Susan Stebbing, *Thinking to some Purpose* (London: Penguin, 1939);

L. Susan Stebbing, *A Modern Elementary Logic* (London: Methuen, 1943; 5th edn., rev. C. W. K. Mundle, 1952).

The two papers in which she first tried to spell out the presuppositions of her own—Moorean—conception of analysis and criticize the logical positivists' conception (as she saw it) are:

L. Susan Stebbing, 'The Method of Analysis in Metaphysics' (1932), *Proceedings of the Aristotelian Society*, 33: 65–94;

L. Susan Stebbing, 'Logical Positivism and Analysis', *Proceedings of the British Academy* (London: British Academy, 1933), pp. 53–87.

Stebbing has been an unduly neglected figure in the history of analytic philosophy, and very little has (yet) been written about her work and influence. But the place to start would be:

Michael Beaney and Siobhan Chapman, 'Susan Stebbing' (2017), *The Stanford Encyclopedia of Philosophy*, <https://plato.stanford.edu/entries/stebbing/>.

I also recommend Chapman's excellent intellectual biography:
Siobhan Chapman, *Susan Stebbing and the Language of Common Sense* (Basingstoke: Palgrave Macmillan, 2013).

Stebbing was a key figure in the so-called Cambridge School of Analysis, on which there is a chapter by Thomas Baldwin ('G. E. Moore and the Cambridge School of Analysis') in the *Oxford Handbook of the History of Analytic Philosophy*.

The Wason selection task and the results of initial tests were first discussed in:

Peter Wason, 'Reasoning', in B. M. Foss (ed.), *New Horizons in Psychology* (London: Penguin, 1966), pp. 135–51;
Peter Wason, 'Reasoning about a rule' (1968), *Quarterly Journal of Experimental Psychology*, 20.3: 273–81.

Plato's famous allegory of the cave can be found in his *Republic* (514a–520a), of which there are many editions and translations readily available. Bacon's trio of similes is quoted from:

Francis Bacon, *The New Organon* (1620), ed. F. H. Anderson (Indianapolis: Bobbs-Merrill, 1960).

Chapter 6: So what is analytic philosophy?

For an account of the various conceptions of analysis in the history of philosophy, see:
Michael Beaney, 'Analysis' (2014), *The Stanford Encyclopedia of Philosophy*, <https://plato.stanford.edu/entries/analysis/>.

The story of Penelope unravelling her web occurs in Book 19 of Homer's *Odyssey* (though, strictly speaking, the Greek verb used is not '*analuein*' but its cognate '*alluein*').

For Carnap's conception of 'explication', which is itself one form of interpretive analysis, see:

Rudolf Carnap, *Logical Foundations of Probability* (Chicago: University of Chicago Press, 1950), ch. 1.

Excluding the texts already cited in the references for the previous chapters, the following texts are mentioned (explicitly or implicitly) in this chapter:

Gilbert Ryle, 'Systematically Misleading Expressions' (1932), in *Collected Essays 1929-1968* (London: Hutchinson, 1971; repr. Abingdon: Routledge, 2009), pp. 41-65;

Gilbert Ryle, *The Concept of Mind* (London: Penguin, 1949);

Gilbert Ryle, 'Phenomenology versus "The Concept of Mind"' (1958), in *Critical Essays* (London: Hutchinson, 1971; repr. Abingdon: Routledge, 2009), pp. 186-204;

J. L. Austin, 'A Plea for Excuses' (1956), in *Philosophical Papers*, 3rd edn., ed. J. O. Urmson and G. J. Warnock (Oxford: Clarendon Press, 1979), pp. 175-204;

J. L. Austin, *How to Do Things with Words*, ed. J. O. Urmson and M. Sbisà (Oxford: Oxford University Press, 1962);

P. F. Strawson, 'On Referring' (1950), in *Logico-Linguistic Papers* (London: Methuen, 1971), pp. 1-27;

P. F. Strawson, *Analysis and Metaphysics: An Introduction to Philosophy* (Oxford: Oxford University Press, 1992);

W. V. Quine, 'Two Dogmas of Empiricism' (1951), in *From a Logical Point of View* (Cambridge, MA: Harvard University Press, 1953), pp. 20-46;

Donald Davidson, 'The Logical Form of Action Sentences' (1967), in *Essays on Actions and Events* (Oxford: Oxford University Press, 1980), pp. 105-22;

Donald Davidson, 'On the Very Idea of a Conceptual Scheme' (1974), in *Inquiries into Truth and Interpretation* (Oxford: Oxford University Press, 1984), pp. 183-98;

Hilary Putnam, 'The Meaning of "Meaning"' (1975), in *Mind, Language and Reality* (Cambridge: Cambridge University Press, 1975), pp. 215-71;

R. G. Collingwood, *An Essay on Philosophical Method* (Oxford: Oxford University Press, 1933);

Bernard Williams, 'Contemporary Philosophy—a Second Look', in N. Bunnin and E. Tsui-James (eds), *The Blackwell Companion to Philosophy* (Oxford: Blackwell, 1996), pp. 25-37;

Jacques Derrida, *Marges de la philosophie* (1972), tr. as *Margins of Philosophy* by Alan Bass (Hemel Hempstead: Harvester, 1982).

For more on these philosophers and their ideas, I recommend the relevant entries in the *Stanford Encyclopedia of Philosophy* (only an entry on Putnam is not yet available) and the chapters in Parts II and III of the *Oxford Handbook of the History of Analytic Philosophy*. Among the most relevant and accessible are the chapters by Hans-Johann Glock ('Wittgenstein's later philosophy'), Maria Baghramian and Andrew Jorgensen ('Quine, Kripke, and Putnam'), Peter Simons ('Metaphysics in analytic philosophy'), Peter Hylton (Ideas of a logically perfect language in analytic philosophy'), P. M. S. Hacker ('The linguistic turn in analytic philosophy'), and Juliet Floyd ('The varieties of rigorous experience'). I address the question 'What is analytic philosophy?' in the first chapter of the *Handbook*, and discuss how analytic philosophy got its name in the second chapter on 'The historiography of analytic philosophy'.

For an account of the Royaumont conference of 1958, see:

Søren Overgaard, 'Royaumont Revisited' (2010), *British Journal for the History of Philosophy*, 18: 899–924.

On the development of historical self-consciousness among analytic philosophers, see:

Erich H. Reck (ed.), *The Historical Turn in Analytic Philosophy* (Basingstoke: Palgrave Macmillan, 2013).

On continental philosophy, there is a readable Very Short Introduction:

Simon Critchley, *Continental Philosophy: A Very Short Introduction* (Oxford: Oxford University Press, 2001).

It was partly this that inspired me to write the present book, to present the 'other side', though I share Critchley's scepticism about the legitimacy and usefulness of talk of a "divide" between 'analytic' and '"continental"' philosophy (with the number of scare quotes here revealing my relative caution concerning the use of these terms!).

Examples of books that have sought to "bridge the gap" include:

Michael Beaney (ed.), *The Analytic Turn: Analysis in Early Analytic Philosophy and Phenomenology* (London: Routledge, 2007);

Mark Textor (ed.), *Judgement and Truth in Early Analytic Philosophy and Phenomenology* (Basingstoke: Palgrave Macmillan, 2013).

Last but by no means least, I strongly recommend the following book for a fuller account of the debates and issues addressed in this chapter:

Hans-Johann Glock, *What is Analytic Philosophy?* (Cambridge: Cambridge University Press, 2008).

I agree with much of what Glock says here, although I would place greater emphasis on the role of analysis in analytic philosophy, especially interpretive analysis and the conceptual creativity it involves. I hope I have shown the importance of this in the present little book.

Index

Index

SOCIAL MEDIA
Very Short Introduction

Join our community
www.oup.com/vsi

- Join us online at the official Very Short Introductions Facebook page.
- Access the thoughts and musings of our authors with our online blog.
- Sign up for our monthly e-newsletter to receive information on all new titles publishing that month.
- Browse the full range of Very Short Introductions online.
- Read extracts from the Introductions for free.
- If you are a teacher or lecturer you can order inspection copies quickly and simply via our website.

ONLINE CATALOGUE
A Very Short Introduction

Our online catalogue is designed to make it easy to find your ideal Very Short Introduction. View the entire collection by subject area, watch author videos, read sample chapters, and download reading guides.

http://global.oup.com/uk/academic/general/vsi_list/